Authentic
Beauty

Authentic *Beauty*

the shaping of a
set-apart young woman

Leslie Ludy

MULTNOMAH
BOOKS

AUTHENTIC BEAUTY
PUBLISHED BY MULTNOMAH BOOKS
12265 Oracle Boulevard, Suite 200
Colorado Springs, Colorado 80921
A division of Random House Inc.

ISBN 978-1-59052-991-1

Published in association with Loyal Arts Literary Agency, LoyalArts.com.

Library of Congress Cataloging-in-Publication Data
Ludy, Leslie.
    Authentic beauty : the shaping of a set-apart young woman / Leslie Ludy. — 1st ed.
        p. cm.
    Includes bibliographical references.
    ISBN 978-1-59052-991-1
    1. Young women—Religious life. I. Title.
    BV4551.3.L83 2007
    248.8'43—dc22

                                    2007003587

Printed in the United States of America
2007—First Edition

10 9 8 7 6 5 4 3 2 1

Contents

Contents

*A*UTHENTIC BEAUTY may very well be one of the rarest earthly treasures today. It holds a magnetism far beyond the loveliness of a properly painted face, and it possesses a charm that towers over the enchanting grace of a sweet personality. It is not ever to be discovered in the pomp and polish of high society, nor in the silk and satin of those conformed to popular culture. Rather, it emerges only rarely in each generation, and that in the life of a young woman—a young woman who is deeply loved by the Prince of her soul.

Authentic
Beauty

Introduction to the Revised Edition

*W*HEN I FIRST began putting words to the message of this book, I pretended that you and I were sitting together in a quaint little coffee shop. We were sipping on our steaming, foamy concoctions, looking each other in the eye, and having a heart-to-heart conversation. For hours and hours, as other customers entered and exited the little shop, we continued talking. We were unaware of time and oblivious to our surroundings. As our coffee mugs slowly emptied, you told me your story. And I told you mine. You shared your questions, struggles, fears, and victories. And I shared mine.

I felt an amazing connection with you as my mind's eye saw us sharing and listening and laughing and crying together. It was the image of our unforgettable time in the cozy coffee shop that inspired the words and style of this book. I pray that as you read each page, you will not feel as if you are reading an impersonal documentary or clinical theory written to the masses. Instead, it is my desire that you will feel as I did when I wrote it—that we are simply two friends, sitting in a coffee shop, having an open, honest, heartfelt talk.

Many of the most poignant examples of cultural influences over my femininity happened at a young age—in high school, middle school, or even younger—so in this book I share quite a few stories from the growing-up years of my life. You may be well past those years of your life as you read about them. You may have experienced things differently than I did growing up. But I hope that the truths and principles illustrated through the stories shared in these pages will speak to you no matter what your age or history. Most of all, it is my prayer that this message will stir within you a longing for Jesus Christ like you have never known before. My hope is that this book will lead you closer to Him than you ever thought you could be. My desire is that the message of this book will impact your life as profoundly as it has mine.

Here are a few details for you to be aware of as you read this book: For the sake of simplicity, when this book refers to our Prince or heavenly Lover, those references are meant to encompass *all* persons of God—the Father, Son, and Holy Spirit. Furthermore, when I present the concept of Jesus being our Lover and Prince, I am referring to a principle clearly presented throughout Scripture of Christ as a Bridegroom and believers as His bride. Indeed, the entire book of Song of Solomon is a poetic expression of this amazing truth.

I am aware that some in our modern times have attempted to pervert this concept into a carnal, twisted, and fleshly idea—referring to an intimate relationship with Christ as if it were a physically sexual relationship rather than a holy spiritual communion. Because of this abuse, some Christians have begun to shy away from the idea of approaching Christ as a Lover or Bridegroom. But to ignore a truth can prove just as dangerous as twisting a truth. If we ignore the Bridegroom attribute of our Lord, we will miss out on the fullness of what it means to have real intimacy with Him.

I hope that, through this book, you will be able to see Jesus Christ in the Lover of your soul, not in a fleshly or physical way, but rather at the spiritual depths of your being, with all reverence and respect. As the great preacher Charles Spurgeon said,

> The music of the Song of Solomon belongs to a higher spiritual life, and has no charm in it for unspiritual ears. The immature may find their carnal and sensuous affections stirred up by it towards Jesus, whom they know "after the flesh" rather than the spirit. The Song occupies a sacred enclosure into which none may enter unprepared. The only ones who can truly understand this love story are those who have attained deep, familiar intimacy with the great Bridegroom.[1]

Let me mention a few practical things before we begin our conversation. Though it is impossible to truly describe the "God experiences" that have taken place in my own life, I have written about them here as if they were actual, word-for-word conversations in hopes of helping translate the concept of interacting with the Spirit of God into simple, everyday language. Additionally, whenever this book uses paraphrased scriptures to make their messages easier to grasp, the actual translations of those scriptures are provided in the endnotes. Also, when necessary, the names of people, places, and some minor details have been altered in order to protect privacy. I should also mention that much of what is shared in these pages is quite candid and thematically mature, so I suggest parental guidance for younger girls who might want to read this book.

Authentic Beauty was first released several years ago, and I have been so incredibly humbled and blessed since then to hear from thousands of young women around the country and the world who have been shaped and inspired by the message of this book. I am especially excited about this new edition, which includes three bonus sections from Eric (my wonderful husband) called "Studying Manhood." Most of us, as young women, have spent a good deal of time in a state of perplexity about the confusing subject of guys, and I have thousands of e-mails and letters from young women to prove it! Why do guys think the way they do? Why do guys treat us the way they do? Why is modern-day manhood so mediocre? These are crucial questions that need to be examined as we seek to discover set-apart femininity.

Eric, like me, has a huge desire to see Christ-centered femininity restored in this culture. He also longs to see Christlike manhood resurrected. And he is convinced that we, as young women, are a vital part of that process. So at three strategic points in the book, we have inserted material from Eric in which he offers his perspective on some of the most common "guy issues" we as modern young women face. These sections are meant to help you understand the world of guys and help transform modern male mediocrity into heroic, Christlike manhood. I hope you will be inspired by them as much as I was.

Several times in this book you will be asked to visit the Web site www.authenticgirl.com. This site includes additional tools you may find helpful, including some bonus material to help you take the message of *Authentic Beauty* even deeper. I would encourage you, if you are able, to take advantage of the valuable resources on this Web site, which have been designed to make the message of this book even more real and practical in your life.

Finally, I would encourage you to use the new companion to this book, *Authentic Beauty: Going Deeper.* This discussion and reflection guide was designed for groups and individuals who want to take this message to the next level in personal application and explore the biblical foundation of the truths discussed within these pages.

I am truly excited to share this journey with you, my friend. So grab your coffee mug, fill it with your favorite drink, pull up a comfortable chair, and let the heart-to-heart adventure begin!

PART I

the first
step

understanding

the

crisis

facing

modern-day

femininity

1

The Erosion of a
Feminine Dream

*I*T HAPPENED WHEN I was six. Somewhere between my encounter with the breathtaking heroine in Walt Disney's *Sleeping Beauty* and my introduction to Malibu Barbie (who came complete with five evening gowns and a hot-pink convertible), I made my decision. Somewhere between watching the lovely Sugar Plum Fairy twirling around on stage during a local production of *The Nutcracker* and trying on my mother's satiny wedding dress, I decided beyond a shadow of a doubt exactly what I wanted to be when I grew up…a beautiful princess.

The fact that princesses were unheard-of in modern-day America did not bother me. I was convinced that somehow, someway, someday

I would become one. It was not that I considered myself especially beautiful or princesslike. In fact, staring into the bathroom mirror one morning at my stringy hair and crooked teeth, I decided that the only remedy was a makeover, which I skillfully applied after digging in my mom's makeup drawer. (The story of my memorable venture out into public that day with my bright pink cheeks, dark green eyelids, and vibrant orange lips is quite an unfortunate tale.) That was the end of my makeup escapades for the time being, but I held out hope that one day I would grow into a dazzling beauty like Cathy Henderson (my all-time favorite baby-sitter), with her supercool, neon pink nail polish and Barbie-like locks.

But much more than polished nails and eternally good hair days, it seemed to me that the *really* necessary requirement for becoming a princess was to find a noble prince: a knight in shining armor who would consider me the most desirable girl in the world, sweep me off my feet, rescue me from peril, carry me away to his castle, and cherish me forever. Sleeping Beauty had Prince Charming. Malibu Barbie had Ken. The Sugar Plum Fairy had the Nutcracker. The Beautiful Bride (a.k.a. my mother) had the Handsome Groom (a.k.a. my father). Even Cathy Henderson had the curly haired Scotty Darnell wrapped around her finger. Finding a prince of my own seemed like a reasonable goal.

It was a childish dream, a girlish desire that budded in my heart long before I knew anything about the real world. But for some inexplicable reason, it was a dream that I longed to come true more than I had ever longed for anything in my entire life. I desperately wanted to become a princess. It was a dream that I treasured, even as I grew older. It was a desire that remained rooted deep within my heart long after Malibu Barbie and her convertible were packed away in Styrofoam peanuts up in the attic. But things were about to change, and change dramatically. In my early childhood innocence, I had no way of knowing the weighty price that would soon be demanded of a young girl who dares to enter the real world holding on to the foolish dream of becoming a princess…

THE DREAM BEGAN to fade when I was ten. I was standing by the water fountain with Mandy and Katie, my two fifth-grade bosom buddies. We were deeply engaged in an animated discussion about the many virtues of Sour Patch Kids, the latest candy craze to hit Crestview Elementary since Nerds had come on the scene a year before. Then, seemingly from out of nowhere, a small group of fifth-grade boys surrounded us, laughing obnoxiously and jolting Mandy out of an awe-inspiring tale of her recent attempt to eat *five* Sour Patch Kids all at the same time. Katie rolled her eyes and looked at the boys in annoyance.

"What do you want?" she demanded.

The ringleader, Andy Archibald, only smirked at Katie. Andy was a loud, skinny kid in baggy Levi's who brought three or four Twinkies in his lunch nearly every day of the week. (I had noticed this fact with great envy, since my mom was a health nut, and the "treats" in my lunchbox were usually carrot sticks and sugar-free granola bars.)

"Go *away*!" Katie ordered in an irritated voice. Andy didn't budge. His sly grin grew wider. He stepped a little closer to her. The rest of the boys began to snicker.

"Timmy *likes* you," Andy finally announced triumphantly, as the snickering grew louder. Timmy immediately shoved Andy against the water fountain, protesting loudly with a swear word. I quickly looked around to see if any teachers had heard him. Fifth graders were not allowed to cuss in school (we were told that once we reached middle school we would be grown up enough to say whatever we wanted in the halls). I expected the Cussing Police to come rushing over, grab

Timmy by the earlobe to drag him off to the principal's office, and force-feed him a bar of Dial. But no adult was anywhere in sight. I found myself strangely disappointed that Timmy's great sin had not created more of a scandal.

My thoughts on this were short-lived, however, because Andy had recovered from Timmy's outburst and seemed to be gaining momentum. "Timmy thinks you're a *babe*," he crooned to Katie in his grating, prepubertized voice, as Timmy yelled, "Shut *up*, dude!"

Katie's face had turned bright red, and she was staring at the floor.

"Yeah," piped in Jason Smits, a squirrelly kid with oversized glasses, "Timmy thinks you're hot, cuz you're *de-vel-op-ing*!" He pointed at Katie's chest. "You have to wear a *training* bra!" At this, the entire group of boys burst into wild, uncontrollable laughter. Katie pursed her lips together in humiliation and hugged her science book tightly against her chest. Mandy glared at the boys but remained speechless. I looked around the hallway again, realizing that there were still no adults anywhere near us to come to the rescue. I decided it was up to me to defend Katie's honor.

"Leave her alone, you jerks!" I burst out. I immediately wished I had kept my mouth shut. The hyper group of boys suddenly turned their full attention on me, and I went from feeling like Wonder Woman to Minnie Mouse in a matter of seconds. Andy curled his lip cynically and looked me up and down.

"Hey," he said, nudging the kid next to him, "check out *this* ugly chick—she's flatter than the plains of Kansas!" The boys howled. Jason quickly opened his mouth to outdo Andy's insult, but before any more verbal abuse could occur, our teacher decided to appear.

"Okay, boys and girls, let's get back in line. Our break is over. It's time for our science lesson!" she called out happily, oblivious to the drama that had just unfolded. The snickering group of boys quickly dispersed, and we were herded into the classroom to learn about the exciting process of metamorphosis.

While Miss Thompson began her lecture on the larval stage of a caterpillar, I was vaguely aware of new, confusing emotions dancing around in my heart. Since I was only ten, I hadn't had much experience being scrutinized, criticized, and discarded by members of the opposite sex. It was a strange sensation, and it created a knot in my stomach that seemed to linger there all afternoon. Andy Archibald's words rang over and over in my ears. It wasn't supposed to work this way, I told myself in bewilderment. There was a marked difference, I noticed, in the way Andy Archibald had treated *me* and the way the beautiful princess was treated by her prince in all the stories I had grown up with. The men in the fairy tales treated women as valuable treasures, to be prized and cherished. The "men" in the fifth grade at Crestview Elementary seemed to treat us the same way they treated their soccer ball—like something to be roughly kicked around for fun, then tossed unnoticed into a corner of the playground.

The longer I sat thinking, the more I found it hard to believe that boys actually *noticed* which girls were wearing training bras and which were still wearing pink cotton undershirts, like me. I had never been insecure about it until that day; in fact, I had never really given it much thought. My friends and I were usually too busy discussing Sour Patch Kids and Care Bears to obsess over our bodies. And until that day by the water fountain, the boys in my class had always spent most of their energy trading baseball cards and telling the latest Pee-wee Herman jokes. But now, they seemed to have found a new, more exciting pastime—tormenting us about how we looked.

Boys like Andy, Timmy, and Jason had always tried to irritate the girls by flipping their eyelids inside out or cracking all their knuckles at once. But now, overnight, they seemed to have realized that they could get a far bigger reaction from us by brutally teasing us about the fascinating new phrases they had learned last week from Miss Thompson in health class. They had started using new words like *developing,* or Katie's most recent downfall, *training bra.* Though Miss Thompson had emphatically explained that these matters were nothing to giggle or be ashamed about, the boys hadn't seemed to catch the part about not laughing. As for not being ashamed about it, I found myself suddenly wanting to ask Miss Thompson how a ten-year-old was *not* supposed to feel embarrassed while facing a group of boys howling about the fact that she had not yet developed. The more I thought about it, the more I became convinced that Miss Thompson and our new workbook called *My Body* were partly to blame for this strange and unwelcome change that had come over the Crestview Elementary fifth-grade boys.

Another possibility I considered might somehow be related was the magazine that Andy Archibald had discovered under his older brother's bed. I had heard Andy telling Jason Smits all about it during Susie Montgomery's oral report on the planet Jupiter a few days before. From what I could tell, it was a magazine with nothing but pictures of women who apparently were not wearing very many clothes, and the boys used the word *babe* repeatedly as they whispered to each other about it. It sounded like a boring magazine to me. I couldn't understand why Andy and Jason were so excited about it. But it had seemed to awaken them to this new idea of studying all the girls and deciding whether or not they were hot.

Whatever was causing the boys to act this way, I knew one thing for sure: being subject to their cruelty was *not* getting me any closer to becoming a princess. In fact, I was beginning to feel more like one of Cinderella's ugly stepsisters than the lovely girl with the glass slipper. A seed of doubt had entered my mind—maybe my dream of becoming a beautiful princess and being cherished by a noble prince was simply not possible for someone like me. Maybe it only happened for girls like Snow White or Malibu Barbie. Maybe men would always see me as ugly and undesirable. Maybe I was not pretty enough, or talented enough, or vivacious enough. Maybe in order to be found attractive...*I* needed to change.

❧ BY THE TIME I was thirteen, thoughts of becoming a princess had all but disappeared from my mind. After three years filled with hundreds of moments like the one by the water fountain at Crestview Elementary, listening to the taunts and barrages of snickering boys who examined and criticized nearly every part of my anatomy, I was tired. Tired of trying to convince myself that someday I would be beautiful. Tired of hoping for a noble prince to rescue me and carry me away to his castle. My desire to be loved and cherished by a gentle knight had not diminished, but had only grown more intense. Yet I had begun to question whether such a fairy tale could ever happen to me. I had innocently stumbled into the real world while holding tightly to my girlish ideals. In response, the world had laughed at my tender heart, mocked my deepest desires, and trampled on my treasured dreams.

Instead of wasting my time looking for a fairy tale, I finally determined that, in order to avoid as much painful rejection as I could, my energy would be better spent on making myself as desirable as possible to the opposite sex. After enduring one too many cynical jabs from greasy-haired boys like Andy, I knew I could not survive that way much longer.

Thankfully, I had become a little more—*ahem*—endowed than in my days at Crestview Elementary. I had also learned a few things by watching other girls around me as they interacted with guys. I decided it was time to put these new tricks into action.

By now the guys had designed a new way of interacting with girls' bodies that went far beyond examining them from a couple feet away. In addition to continually scrutinizing and graphically describing our bodies, they had also developed the habit of attempting to grab, touch, and tickle anything feminine that ignited their hormones. How a girl responded to these gestures often determined the way she was treated from that point on.

One morning during my first week of eighth grade, as I was rummaging through the chaos in the bottom of my bright orange locker, I had an eye-opening experience. My friend Ashley had the locker next to mine, and she was passionately describing to me the horrors of Ms. Vickers (her militaristic English teacher) as she tried to shove a notebook into her already overflowing backpack. Suddenly, she was cornered by Matt Montoya and Tyler Pierce, two wiry basketball players with spiked hair and oversize shorts that showed off a good five inches of their boxers.

"Hey, babe, how about a quickie in the bathroom?" Matt panted into Ashley's ear as Tyler stood behind her and unhooked her bra through her Hard Rock Café T-shirt.

I pretended to be captivated by the cover of my social studies book, but I watched the scene closely out of the corner of my eye. Instead of staring helplessly at the floor with a red face or angrily protesting in the name of sexual harassment, Ashley had a different and surprising reaction.

"Ma-a-tt!" she squealed, playfully pushing him away and giggling. Then she spun around with an affectionately annoyed smile at Tyler, who was just beginning to tug at the back of her jeans.

"*Stop* it," she whined in a cute, lighthearted voice, looking up at him seductively as she skillfully rehooked her bra.

Matt was not to be ignored. "Come on, Ash," he crooned, sliding his hands down past her belt, "just five minutes—you and me?"

At that moment, the bell shrieked loudly from a speaker above us, and the steamy dialogue dissolved. With one last pinch near Ashley's back pocket, Matt slung his backpack over his arm, and he and Tyler strutted down the hall, laughing obnoxiously as they glanced back over their shoulders at Ashley, who was grinning back at them.

I learned quickly. It seemed to me that the girls who responded to guys the way Ashley did knew exactly what they were doing. Instead of getting ridiculed and mocked by guys, they got drooled over, touched, and propositioned. Maybe this wasn't the ideal kind of male attention. Still, it was far less painful than complete humiliation and rejection, which is exactly what a girl would get if she showed any sign of resistance to their constant sexual attention. We had been taught in health class about the importance of standing up to sexual harassment and were told that we should not hesitate to come to any adult if we were being verbally assaulted at school. But this advice was so pathetically impractical, it was quickly tossed aside. What girl wanted to invite even more ridicule and torment by drawing attention to the fact that she was upset by the way the guys were treating her?

I soon mastered Ashley's technique—laughing carelessly when guys attempted to unbutton my shirt during boring class lectures, flirting playfully when they tried to touch me in the hall, joking back effortlessly when they made sexual comments to me on the bus— although none of it came naturally. But soon I was giggling, teasing, and seducing right along with the best of them. Ashley had taught me well. And she was right—this new approach was ten times better than silently enduring the cruel taunts of greasy-haired boys or trying to fight back with their sarcastic laughter ringing in my ears.

There was another apparent advantage as well: whenever a guy like Matt or Tyler would hover around my locker, sliding his hands into the back pockets of my jeans or toying with my bra strap, I felt a newfound freedom from a nagging fear. It was a fear that had haunted me since that unforgettable moment in the hall with Andy

Archibald during my fifth-grade year. I was finally able to convince myself that maybe, just maybe, I wasn't ugly or undesirable after all. No matter how different Matt and Tyler were from my childhood dreams of a knight in shining armor, at least through their flirtatious attention I could dull the longing that had started in the fifth grade: to be found attractive in the eyes of the opposite sex.

🦋 I HEARD IT first from Vinny Rigaletti, a short kid with red hair and braces who wore black Umbros and Body Glove T-shirts every single day of the year.

"Brandon's breaking up with Stephanie. He's gonna ask you out tonight," he whispered conspiratorially over my terminal in the computer lab. I gazed back at Vinny with all the steely indifference of 007, but my heart was hammering inside my chest like the Energizer Bunny after five Mountain Dews. Without realizing it, Vinny had just announced the beginning of a significant new chapter in my young life.

It was the middle of my eighth-grade year, and it seemed I had finally reached a new level. Instead of my merely being a sex object toyed with in the halls, now a guy actually *liked* me. Brandon was a tall, blond-haired, blue-eyed athlete with an irresistible smile. (My friends said he looked almost exactly like Vanilla Ice, which at that time was actually a compliment.) The fact that Brandon apparently liked *me* enough to break up with Stephanie—a dark-haired beauty who looked like a walking Gap ad—completely baffled me. It amazed me. It flattered me.

That night when the phone rang and I heard Brandon's soft voice declaring his unfailing love for me, a faltering hope entered my heart. It was a hope that I hadn't entertained for years, and even now it was only a flicker. Could it possibly be that my childhood dream to be cherished by a noble knight in shining armor was about to come true?

For the first few weeks of my relationship with Brandon, it seemed like the answer to that wondering was a resounding yes. Brandon treated me the way no other guy ever had—like I was truly valuable to him. He wrote me romantic notes nearly every day, then stuffed them into my locker or my notebooks for me to find. He waited for me after almost every class and tenderly wrapped his arm around me as we walked down the hall together. Every night, Brandon would call me as soon as he finished dinner and remind me how much he was in love with me. The girlhood dream of becoming a beautiful princess, treasured by an adoring prince, began to reawaken in my heart.

In the fairy tales, when a princess was cherished by a valiant prince, she gave up everything to follow him to the ends of the earth. Snow White gave up her cute little cottage with the cute little dwarfs; Sleeping Beauty gave up her comfortable bed, pj's, and never-ending slumber; and the Little Mermaid gave up her mer-family, her special fins that allowed her to race with the dolphins, and her extremely cool underwater caves—all for the men of their dreams. In every story, the princess and her prince lived happily ever after. Now that I had finally found a prince who loved me and found me beautiful, I knew that in order to keep his devoted love, I too would have to give him something. And I knew what that something must be—my heart.

It wasn't a hard task. Since most of the time I was walking on a cloud, basking in the amazement of Brandon's adoration for me, giving my heart to him came effortlessly. As the months raced by, I began to build my life around him. He was the first person I would rush to meet the moment I got to school, the one I would spend every spare moment of my day with, the occupation of nearly all my thoughts and daydreams, the last voice I would listen to before drifting off to sleep, and the face that would appear in my mind as soon as I awakened in the morning.

Soon it became unusual for me to walk alone through a crowded hallway, it felt strange to eat lunch without him sitting next to me, and I became unsettled and restless if a night ever passed without hearing his voice on the other end of the phone. The week Brandon came down with pneumonia and couldn't be with me every waking hour of my day or remind me of his affection by phone at night, I realized with startling clarity that I could not live without him. Brandon had become my life. Since Brandon had made it clear that I had become *his* life, giving my heart to him completely did not seem like a sacrifice. Surely he would always cherish it. I was finally on my way to becoming a princess.

❧ WHEN THE FAIRY tale began to crumble, it was almost too subtle for me to notice that it was happening. It was just a handful of little things here and there—catching Brandon's gaze lingering on a pretty girl in the hall or walking into the cafeteria to find him in a lively tickling match with a couple of cute cheerleaders. I soon had the sickening suspicion that his love was slipping away from me. The devastating realization that if he left he would take my heart with him began to gnaw at me day and night.

My solution was not to guard what was left of my heart, but rather to give him every remaining shred of it in a last-ditch effort to entice him to stay. I wrote him desperate letters baring my soul, made him romantic gifts that declared my undying love, and even allowed him to take nearly everything I had to give of my body. Nothing worked. He was shattering my dream, and I was powerless to stop him.

The pain of Brandon's rejection was far more intense and overwhelming than Andy Archibald's fifth-grade cruelty. Brandon had been my salvation, a prince who had finally rescued me, allowing me to believe that my lifelong dream of becoming a princess was coming true. And then, like a shocking horror movie in which the hero morphs into the villain, he had transformed from a prince into a monster. He had destroyed my delicate heart—a gift I had willingly and trustingly offered him. The fairy tale had taken a nightmarish turn. I racked my brain but could remember no example of a time something like this ever happened to the princesses in my childhood stories.

When the tumultuous waves of our breakup began to subside, I discovered that I had drastically changed. I was left emotionally bleeding, desperate, and helpless. Before Brandon, my longing to be a cherished princess was simply a fading childhood dream. But strangely, now that my young heart had been trampled and crushed, this childhood longing became an unquenchable thirst. I knew that from that point on, I simply could not survive without finding it. It was the only way to ease the unbearable pain I now carried with me daily. I felt like a delicate flower that had been plucked from its life source. I knew I was on the verge of withering up and dying if I did not quickly find something to nourish my exposed heart.

I looked for it in other relationships. My status as Brandon's ex-girlfriend had elevated me to the popularity level where other guys started showing interest in me. So I gave myself to one after another. Though my parents' advice, conventional wisdom, and even the lovely ladies in the fairy tales had always taught me that men preferred women who allowed the *guy* to be the aggressive one, that was not the message I received from the world I lived in. Guys in my world seemed to value only girls who initiated relationships, flirting, and sex—girls who had absolutely no boundaries around their hearts or bodies. At the age of fifteen, I found myself being molded into the kind of girl the world expected me to be.

The next season of my life was the most hellish I have ever experienced. My desperate searching for a prince who would cherish me forever had become my demise. I had listened to the voice of the culture and become the young woman it convinced me to be, hoping that the result would be the discovery of a happily-ever-after tale. Instead, my heart was mercilessly trampled time and time again. My body was used for the animalistic gratification of guys who were as far from being gallant knights as Gumby is from being the Incredible Hulk. One by one, my precious dreams were shattered beyond recognition.

I WAS NOT the only girl surviving this kind of miserable existence. I became aware of this fact through many experiences, such as the night I was lounging on a brown shag couch with a supersize package of Starbursts in Jody Smith's basement. Seven or eight girls were sprawled on the floor or on couches, and I was silently listening to their midnight banter as I unwrapped a strawberry cube and let it slowly dissolve in my mouth. (Chewing was out of the question, due to my orthodontist's twisted pursuit to tighten my braces beyond the point of cruel and unusual punishment.)

"Kelly, just answer one question—why the @#$%! did you fool around with Nathan last night? You *know* he's totally in love with Elizabeth Yates." The blunt question was posed by Amy Wilhelm, a hyper volleyball player with an unyielding, and often annoying, curiosity streak.

Kelly was a blond cheerleader with a perpetual tan. She ripped open a bag of Doritos and rolled her eyes. "I don't give a $#%@ who he's in love with—he's hot!" Kelly replied passionately, shoving two chips into her mouth and crunching down on them loudly. "And he's a really good kisser," she added between bites. Kelly would know—

she had slept with nearly every varsity football player, fluttering from one to the next like a honeybee in a flower garden. I always admired her couldn't-care-less attitude every time she got dumped by a guy who had just used her. She seemed to be able to shut off her emotions like a light switch.

But now, as I watched her go through an entire bag of Doritos in three minutes, I saw something in her eyes I had never seen before. Hopelessness. I realized that Kelly was seeking the same thing I was—to be loved and cherished unconditionally. Like me, she had been hurt too many times to believe it was possible. But maybe every time she was in the arms of a new guy, if only for a night, she could pretend she was valued. Though I wasn't exactly a one-night-stand kind of girl, I could relate to that feeling.

"Hey, did you guys hear that Laney Jackson tried to kill herself?" piped up Jody suddenly.

"Who's Laney Jackson?" Kelly asked in a bored voice.

"You know, that girl in our geometry class—the one who was dating Alex Chamberlain?" Jody reminded her, reaching for a can of Pepsi.

"Oh yeah, I know who you're talking about! Didn't she, like, try to OD on her mom's painkillers the day he dumped her?" Amy charged back into the conversation, clearly excited to be chewing on this succulent new morsel of gossip.

I thought about the abyss of despair I had spiraled into when Brandon broke up with me. I could almost imagine the devastation Laney felt when Alex smashed her heart into thousands of pieces. I could picture her hopeless face as she slowly opened the bottle of little white pills. Another princess who had been rejected by the prince she thought would always love her.

I looked around the room at the girls. They weren't much different from the hundreds of girls I encountered every day at school or even at church. There seemed to be a remnant of shattered princess dreams in each of them. And none of them seemed remotely close to having that dream come true.

Amy was animatedly chattering about the Alex-Laney scandal, and I started to wonder if her obsession with the juicy details of other people's lives was a front to keep us from asking any questions about her own. I had heard from Jody that Amy's father had molested her from the time she was seven. It occurred to me that Amy's dream of becoming a princess was most likely annihilated by her father before it ever really began. So here she was, creating drama wherever she could find it, focusing on other people's pain so she would be too busy to feel her own.

"Oh, #$%!" Jody suddenly swore. "How many Pepsis have I had? Man! I *cannot* have any more calories this week or there is no way I'll be able to do the swimsuit shoot on Saturday!" She shoved the half-empty Pepsi can away in disgust.

"Jody, *please*. You haven't eaten a meal since Thursday," Kelly said impatiently. "If you stay on this pathetic lettuce and grapefruit diet, you're gonna start passing out in the hall every other day like you did last year."

Jody, in her spare time, was a teen model who frequently appeared in local department store ads in the weekend newspapers. She had an avid male following at our school, and she was terrified of losing her modeling status and, thus, the devoted attention and approval of so many guys. Her room was covered with posters of Victoria's Secret models and pinups from *Sports Illustrated* swimsuit issues to constantly remind her of what she needed to look like and, presumably, motivate her not to eat. She was tall and elegant, but painfully thin, and her new goal was to drop from a size 4 down to a 2. Jody had been hospitalized twice for anorexia. She must have convinced herself that in order to receive the kind of love and approval she had always wanted, she couldn't stop until she withered into the body of a wraithlike supermodel.

Later that night, as the final credits from the latest Hollywood chick flick danced across Jody's big-screen television, we lay on the floor sighing and talking wistfully. The movie's brave and sensitive hero was the epitome of our ultimate knight-in-shining-armor fantasies. But that's all it was—a movie—and we knew it. I realized we had all surrendered to the fact that the only place that we could ever hope or expect to find a noble prince who would truly love and cherish his princess was in the comforting unreality of Hollywood. If no other girl had found even a hint of what I had been after since childhood, then it was time to stop kidding myself. My dream of becoming a princess would never come true.

2

The Reviving of the Feminine Heart

*L*OOKING BACK ON my life, I see how far I strayed from my childhood, fairy-tale ideals. I see how tarnished and torn I became on my quest to become a cherished princess. Because of that, I am amazed at what ultimately happened on my journey. After years of heartache and despair, I stumbled upon a path I never before knew existed. Trekking through the rugged terrain of life, I had been blinded to its presence by my pain. But when I finally allowed myself to take a tentative step onto this ancient, dusty, hidden path, my entire world was altered. And miraculously, my wounded feminine heart, with all its disillusionment and disappointment, was revived.

After years of convincing myself that all my searching for love had been in vain, a most unusual thing happened. I discovered my prince. All of my confusing female desires and seemingly foolish princess dreams now found their purpose…in him. This love story did not happen merely because of an amazing stroke of good fortune. It did not occur simply because I happened to be in the right place at the right time. This beautiful romance was made possible by something far more tangible, something that lies within the grasp of every young woman. The following account of the love story I discovered may seem like a surreal daydream, but it is far closer to reality than you might guess. So please don't be tempted to write it off as unattainable. Your feminine heart may be much closer to finding true love than you think.

�֍ HE WAS SOMEONE I had known for years. He had been a close family friend. He had many appealing qualities, but I had never really thought about him in a romantic way. It was true that he had a sensitive and tender side that I had seen on a few occasions. But he was also extremely passionate about truth, and I felt that sometimes he came across a little too strong on certain points. To be honest, he intimidated me. It also seemed that he was a little too involved with "church stuff." When I thought of him, I was reminded of Sunday-school lessons with flannel Bible story characters or gold offering plates—this was not exactly the atmosphere for true love!

He was one of those people with a piercing gaze who can see straight into the depths of your soul. Because of this, I had gone out of my way to avoid him for the past few years. For some time now, my life had been a chaotic mess of compromise and confusion. I didn't want him to see what I had become. If he found out what I had done, I was sure he would sternly reprimand me and remind me that

it was too late for me to ever discover anything more. But I soon realized I was very, *very* wrong about him.

I found him waiting for me by the apple trees near my back gate
one day as I headed out for a morning walk. I was startled to see him
there, surprised that, after all these years and all the times I had
ignored him, he still wanted to spend time with me. I gave him a tentative glance, and he smiled at me—a tender, intimate smile that
made my heart lurch in spite of itself. I quickly looked away.

"Can I walk with you?" he asked in a gentle voice. I nodded, still
avoiding his gaze, and he fell into step beside me. We made our way
in silence for a while, listening to the occasional chatter of a squirrel
or high-pitched chirp of a robin. I kept my eyes on the gravel path at
my feet.

"I missed you," he told me simply. Though it was obvious to both
of us that *I* was the one who had put the distance between us, there
was no hint of accusation in his tone. I bit my lip and nodded again,
unsure what to say in response.

We walked a little farther, and I realized his presence was both
refreshing and comforting. I could feel his tender eyes watching me,
silently telling me how important I was to him, though I could not
figure out why. Nothing else was said during the rest of our time
together that day, but I sensed that something more was about to happen between us. I just wasn't sure if I was ready.

Our friendship slowly grew. The more time I spent with him, the
more I realized how different he was from any man I had ever
encountered. In him, there were none of the sex-hungry glances I had
received from the guys at school, not a trace of the flirtatious teasing
that had come to surround me, and not a strain of the seductive
charms I had grown so accustomed to in men. But somehow I knew
that he loved me. That he deeply desired me. That he found me beautiful. I hardly dared to hope that I had finally found the one man who

could fulfill those long-forgotten dreams of mine. Even if he could be my prince, I was sure I had found him too late.

"This is completely crazy," I told myself aloud one night as I tossed and turned in bed. "He wouldn't want someone like me." I was convinced that his love for me would shrivel up in a second if he truly understood how many mistakes I had made. I didn't think I could risk becoming attached to him. I had been hurt so many times that I didn't know how much more pain my heart could handle.

I had another worry. He didn't live his life the way anyone else did. He stood out like a neon billboard on a lonely desert highway. He was mocked and misunderstood by quite a few people in my life. I knew he would not fit into my world, would not be accepted by my friends, and would not be at home in most of my surroundings. How could I possibly love someone like this? What did he expect me to do—walk away from everything just to be with him?

I wrestled with my fears for weeks. He never pressured me to make a decision. He simply reminded me, in a hundred different ways, that he loved me and that he longed for me. He was infinitely patient, tender, and sensitive...the kind of prince I had dreamed of for as long as I could remember. He made the immature romantic wannabes who had historically gained my affection seem like pitiful counterfeits. After seeing the real thing, I couldn't believe I had fallen for such poor substitutes. But at the same time, I couldn't help wondering whether or not he might just be too good to be true.

The more time I spent around him, the more something inside me desperately wanted to just surrender and fall into his waiting arms. But I was afraid to let myself trust him. I was afraid of what that decision might cost me.

Over time, gradually, like the moving of the hour hand, my guard came down. No matter how many times I pulled away from him, his love remained unmoving, like a majestic, unwavering mountain overlooking a tumultuous ocean. I had even tried to convince him that I was not good enough for him. I'd told him in detail, with hot tears flashing in my tormented eyes, exactly what I had done with my life, heart, and body over the past years. But I sensed that instead of judging me, he was inwardly weeping over every piece of my shattered heart. Coming face to face with this infinite kindness left me stunned.

One morning, as I was sitting alone on a bench in the crisp spring air, I felt him softly approach me. He didn't have to speak. I took a long look into the depths of love in his eyes, and I melted. With tears coursing down my face, I fell into his arms and told him passionately that my heart belonged to no one but him. At that moment, my life, my pursuits, my friends, everything I had built my world around faded away into nothingness. None of it seemed even remotely important anymore. Nothing mattered now but him.

As I whispered my devotion to him, a brilliant peace crept into my heart and began to mend its broken pieces. His eyes were wet with tears of joy. I felt like an eagle gliding along the majestic mountain peaks following an afternoon storm. *I had finally found my prince.* He had gallantly searched for me and rescued me from my dungeon of captivity. He had loved me in spite of my wretched, ugly condition. He had taken the filthy rags I was clothed in and given me the sparkling gown of a beautiful princess. His amazing love had fully revived my shattered, wounded, bleeding heart. And though I knew that I must now sacrifice all I had ever known in order to be with him, there was not a shred of doubt lingering in my mind. It was like giving him a pile of worthless pebbles and receiving a houseful of priceless jewels in return.

OVER THE PAST several years, I have interacted with thousands of young women my age. Rarely have I met one who didn't relate to my childhood longing to become a beautiful princess. Whether we grew up wanting to sing like Orphan Annie, save galaxies like Princess Leia, or rescue helpless victims like Wonder Woman; whether we were tree-climbing tomboys with skinned knees or tea-pouring cherubs in ringlets; whether our ambitions in life were to run a household or run the United States—there seems to be a bond we share, a deep, unshakable, intrinsic longing to be tenderly cherished forever by a noble prince to whom we may entrust our hearts. We long to experience the kind of breathtaking love we read about in fairy tales, hear about in love songs, or see unfold on movie screens. Most of us would even be willing to give up everything we hold dear just to ride away into the sunset with the man of our dreams.

But we live in a culture that is out to destroy all such dreams with a vengeance. Most of us are incredibly young and naive when our innocent hopes are trampled, whether by an abusive father, a divorce-riddled family, a merciless sex predator, or simply the cruel taunts of our classmates. Wounded and desperate, we embark upon a search to find value, to find someone who will accept us, approve us, cherish us, and tell us we are beautiful.

Growing up, I was privileged enough to have a wonderful mom and dad who reminded me often that I was special and loved. Many girls aren't so blessed. But even with the positive influence of my parents, I gradually allowed the culture to convince me that in the eyes of the world I was considered worthless and ugly.

Almost every young woman I meet has, to some degree, bought into this same lie. Like I did, many young women willingly offer their hearts, their emotions, or their bodies to anyone who seems like he might somehow fulfill that deep longing within—only to be used and violated and left holding shattered dreams. Others starve themselves or willingly become sex toys in the hope that, by doing so, they might be found beautiful and valuable. Some simply give up all hope and decide it is not worth trying anymore—they plunge into depression or drivenness and keep the pain buried under the surface for as long as they possibly can.

We live in a world that seeks to destroy all that is princesslike and feminine within us. From a very young age, our world mocks any longing for tender romance or true love that might linger in our hearts. Our culture tells us that instead of dreaming about giving our hearts to some mythical knight in shining armor, we would be far wiser to spend our time looking out for ourselves. From the time we are ten years old (or younger in many cases), teachers like Miss Thompson turn the female body into a scientific chart, inform us that sexuality is nothing but an animalistic impulse, and scoff at any of us who would dare dream that there could be more. Little boys who might otherwise be preoccupied with baseball cards and G.I. Joes learn—whether from health class, television, classmates, or their dads and older brothers—that in order to become "men" they must examine, objectify, critique, and lust after girls' bodies while acting out their animalistic sexual urges.

Sadie, a frustrated college sophomore, wrote me an e-mail not too long ago that included this statement: "This may sound crazy, but I am starting to get the feeling that every guy I meet is only spending time with me because he wants to use my body."

Unfortunately, that does not sound crazy. It sounds like reality. No wonder so many young women are settling for broken hearts and shattered dreams. In today's world, it can be nearly impossible for us to believe that there could ever be anything more.

A spunky brunette named Carrie told me recently, "Leslie, it's not fair! You married the last true knight in shining armor on the planet! No more exist!"

I have heard that statement countless times from young women. When they observe my relationship with Eric (my adorable husband)

31

or hear about the romance of our love story, it strikes them as so unusual that they begin to wonder if another man like him can ever be found.

Yes, Eric and I *did* have an amazing love story (in fact, Anne Shirley and Gilbert Blythe—of *Anne of Green Gables* fame—don't stand a chance against us!). However, my love story with Eric is only a *small* reflection of a much deeper intimacy that I share with *someone else*…the Prince I wrote about earlier. The One who was waiting for me that morning by the apple trees when I went out for my walk. The One I surrendered to on that unforgettable spring morning a few months later. The One who passionately loved me, tenderly held me, and deeply cherished me in a way I had never before experienced, in a way that fulfilled all my childhood longings and desires. The One who rescued me from the dingy prison cell I had wandered into, cut the iron chains away from my feet and hands, tenderly washed me clean from my life of sin, transformed me into His princess, and carried me away into the sunset to His land.

My true Prince is not Eric. *My true Prince is Jesus Christ.* Eric, with all his amazing qualities, could never meet the deepest needs inside my heart the way my true Prince has. If not for the tender love of my true Prince, my love story with Eric would not have even been possible. The romance of my love story with Eric is only a faded glimmer of the spectacular beauty of the love story I share with my Jesus Christ. In fact, my childhood longing to be loved and cherished by a tender knight that I could follow to the ends of the earth was placed in my heart by Him. Jesus Christ alone can fulfill that desperate longing.

Many of us think we know Jesus Christ. We mention Him often in conversation, visit Him at church once or twice a week, read our Bibles periodically so we can understand Him better, and maybe even declare that He is our number-one priority in life. But just as there is a marked distinction between memorizing the definition of *rose* in *Webster's* dictionary and actually holding one in your hand, there is a huge difference between *saying* you know Jesus Christ and actually *experiencing* Him as your *true Prince,* your Hero, and the One you give up everything just to be with.

So many of us, though we claim to know Jesus Christ, are still longing for our deepest desires to be fulfilled by someone else. We frantically seek the man of our dreams, giving ourselves completely to one relationship after the next, hoping that when we finally find the right guy our romantic fantasies will become reality.

"Jesus Christ is your *true Prince,*" I often say to young women, "the One who gave His very life just to be with you, the One who can rescue you from the dungeon you are in, the One who can transform you into a radiant princess, the One who can carry you away to His beautiful land to cherish you forever. He is the only One who can meet your deepest longings; He is the only One worthy of your entire heart, life, soul, and body—all you are and all you have. *Jesus Christ is the Prince* you should passionately pursue with all your heart."

"Yeah, sure, okay, whatever," is the typical response, followed by, "but there's this *guy* I met…"

Most of us don't ever realize that Jesus Christ is not a flimsy, flannel-board figure from a Sunday-school lesson; that He is not a stern dictator looking down on us from heaven to make sure we obey His rules; that He is not a distant being who is too busy running the world to care about the details of our day-to-day lives; and that He is so much more than someone we say we believe in to keep ourselves out of hell when we die.

He is the Lover of our souls. Our true Prince. The One we have been longing for, searching for, and dreaming of since childhood. The One who will love us the way no one else can love us; the One who will cherish us forever; the One who will transform us from hopeless girls in rags into beautiful, confident, radiant princesses. He is the One who makes us ready for true, lasting, *human* love. And He is the One who meets our deepest needs when human love falls short.

In every generation, there are a few young women who discover their true Prince. Just like the princesses in my childhood fairy tales, once they meet this Prince and realize His incredible love for them, they *willingly give up everything else* to follow Him to the ends of the earth. They live lives with their Prince that are utterly different from the world around them. They are radiant. They are confident. They are fulfilled. They possess a truly authentic beauty that flows from within. They are world changers. They are set apart in complete and utter devotion to their Prince. And they stand out from among all other young women like lilies among thorns.

This book is an invitation for *you* to become one of those few in *this* generation: a set-apart young woman who allows the passionate intimacy she experiences with her Prince to completely transform every area of her life.

No matter how many times our dreams have been shattered, or how many times our hearts have been trampled, or how far we have strayed from Him, our Prince is standing outside our dungeon windows, patiently waiting for us to hear His voice and invite Him to rescue us from the bleakness of a life lived without Him.

This kind of fairy-tale romance between a young woman and her true Prince does not come without sacrifice. It does not come without pain. But it is the most priceless gift we will ever be offered. And it is the most beautiful and fulfilling existence we could ever imagine.

lily among *thorns*

the essence

of a set-apart

young woman

Like a lily among the thorns,
so is my darling among the maidens.

SONG OF SOLOMON 2:2

3

Lily White

Beginning the Set-Apart Life

*Jesus made it clear to His disciples that if they would come away
with Him, they first must forgo their personal life agendas,
say good-bye to all that they prize and are comforted by in
this life, and then, and only then, follow Him.*

MATTHEW 16:24, PARAPHRASE[2]

*O*UR PERCEPTION OF our femininity is often shaped by the culture in which we live when we are still very young. Reflecting back on my growing-up years, I can recall certain defining moments—little experiences that subtly altered my thinking and also stealthily changed my course. Take, for instance, one of the few memorable "guy conversations" I was exposed to during my freshman year of high school...

Trampled Innocence

I was sitting in the school cafeteria, staring blankly at my geometry textbook during a free class period. Three popular guys were sitting a few tables away from me, bantering back and forth in a lively conversation. Keeping my eyes glued to the giant octagon on page twenty-four, I strained my ears to hear what they were saying.

I was less than awe inspired by what I heard. The guys were trying to impress each other with their latest batting averages or bench-press weights (which all seemed to me to have been grossly inflated). Then they moved on to declaring—with *Die Hard* toughness—which hotshot jock's, um, "gluteus maximus" they were going to kick at Saturday's game. This was followed by a highly sophisticated and competitive burping contest. Soon my geometry textbook began to seem as appealing as a sunny beach vacation in contrast to this mind-numbing pubescent banter. But then things suddenly took an interesting turn.

"Did you *see* Karly Colson yesterday?" Trevor Simms asked his buddies, interrupting Justin Maxwell's burped rendition of the letter *N* as he attempted to work his way through the alphabet. Immediately, Justin's lofty burping goals were forgotten, and he eagerly joined in the far more exhilarating report on the many curves of Karly Colson's perfectly proportioned body.

I was used to guys graphically discussing girls' bodies—I heard it nearly every day at school. But something was different about *this* conversation. Without a girl around, the guys seemed to rise to a whole new level of perversion. As Trevor and Justin launched into a shocking description of exactly what they would like to be doing to Karly, my cheeks began to flush and I realized I was holding my breath in disbelief. What I was hearing was so horrifically graphic and twisted that I started to wonder if they were reading the script from a porn video.

They moved on to dissect other girls—many of them my

friends—in the same disgusting way they had talked about Karly. I sat frozen in horror and embarrassment. My mind was racing with bewilderment. This didn't make sense. Trevor and Justin had never struck me as sex crazed. They even seemed a little more clean cut and respectful than most guys. They frequently showed up at our church's youth group on Wednesday nights. They were smart, funny, and athletic, made good grades, and didn't do drugs or get drunk on weekends. It was hard for me to comprehend how guys like Trevor and Justin could see girls as nothing more than juicy pieces of meat.

As the conversation continued, I noticed something else that perplexed me. The guys seemed especially impressed with any girl who had no sense of shame in sleeping around. The looser she was, the more attractive she was to them.

"Dude, Shannon Walters is so awesome—she had sex with five different guys at Kyle's party last night."

"Yeah, but check this out, dude—Angela Elliot's gonna do a threesome with Todd McDonald and Danny Whitehall!"

"Are you *serious,* dude? Man, she *rocks!*"

They were utterly disdainful of girls who had different standards.

"Yeah, Rachel Edmonds is really hot, but she's a total prude, man. She's one of those pure, religious girls. She has to wear those cast-iron bras and panties that have a lock and key, just so no guy can ever get to her." They burst into obnoxious laughter at Rachel's ridiculous reluctance to lose her virginity.

My shock had reached its boiling point, and I found myself wishing I could rush over to them and demand an explanation for their debased behavior. But at that moment, the overhead bell squawked shrilly, and the guys quickly disbanded, leaving one another with a round of smooth high fives and fist bangs. For the next several hours, I couldn't get their lustful words out of my mind. Up until then, I had limited the extent of fifteen-year-old male perversion to their immature sexual advances, like the scene at Ashley's locker on my first day of eighth grade. But what I heard in the cafeteria that day made me wonder if I had underestimated the depth of their sexual obsessions.

My last class of the day was Spanish, and I noticed that, in an amazing stroke of good fortune, Trevor Simms (one of the perverted conversation participants) had taken the seat behind me. I had met Trevor once or twice at youth group but didn't know him very well. Typically, I wouldn't have felt comfortable striking up a conversation with someone of such marginal acquaintance. But now my indignation was making me bold. I was dying to tell him that I had overheard the disgusting way he had described my friends' bodies. I wanted to see him red faced with shame over the fact that I had peered into the caverns of his lewd mind. As soon as Mr. Alvarez left us with our worksheets on basic Spanish verbs, I saw my opportunity.

"So," I ventured, turning around casually, "you think Karly Colson's hot, don't you?"

Trevor frowned, eyeing me suspiciously. "What are you talking about?"

"I heard you guys talking this morning in I.A.," I announced. (I.A. was short for the Industrial Arts cafeteria—the standard on-campus hangout for anybody who was considered even remotely cool.)

"Okay, whatever," Trevor recovered from his surprise and quickly shrugged it off as if he couldn't care less. He mindlessly scrawled on his worksheet and tried to ignore me. But I was on a mission.

"You are a total pervert, you know," I suddenly lashed out.

Trevor's head came up sharply, and he glared at me in annoyance. "What the &%#@ is your problem?"

"No, what is *your* problem?" I shot back furiously. "Do you think all girls are just sex objects?"

Trevor's face turned red, and he started squirming uncomfortably in his chair.

"*Well?*" I demanded, enjoying his awkwardness.

Trevor's face got redder. "Um, yes! I mean, no! I mean, um, well, I don't know!" He was wiggling like a worm stranded on the sidewalk after a storm. I remained silent for a moment, gloating in my triumph over this cocky heartthrob who normally exuded nothing but suave coolness. I was sure I had just done a huge favor for women everywhere by exposing his debased attitude toward the female anatomy.

But when I glanced back at Trevor, to my surprise, his face was no longer red and he was no longer squirming uncomfortably. In fact, he seemed to have gained a mysterious confidence. I noticed that his eyes had formed into a haughty squint as he studied me.

"Listen, Leslie," he began patronizingly, "you need to get a clue about something, okay? This is just the way guys are! Why do you even care? Girls do the same thing to guys! It's not something to get all upset over. I mean, don't take this the wrong way, but you're acting like my *mom* or something. Girls who have a cow about stuff like this are kind of a turnoff, you know? Just be cool about it."

I stared at him in silence. His words had somehow turned the tables. Suddenly, instead of being charged with anger, I felt embarrassed by my emotional tirade. The last thing I wanted was to be a turnoff or act like anybody's mom. The thought of Trevor and all his friends mocking my misguided female protests made me blush with humiliation. Maybe I *was* the only girl around who would actually get up in arms over this kind of thing. Maybe, as Trevor had implied, I was just being old fashioned and prudish. I decided then and there that I could not let myself become known as the out-of-touch, mom-like chick from Trevor's Spanish class. Swallowing hard, I mumbled something that conveyed reluctant agreement. But long after Mr. Alvarez had polished off his fascinating exposé on Spanish verbs, I sat pondering Trevor's confident declaration. "*This is just the way guys are.*"

✖ MY PARENTS HAD always exhorted me with statements like "Boys don't like easy girls" or "Boys have respect for the girls who wait." But according to what I had heard that morning in the I.A. cafeteria, easy girls like Shannon Walters or Angela Elliot were the only girls guys really wanted. Girls like Rachel, who chose to wait, were of no value whatsoever, it seemed, other than to become the brunt of guys' hilarious cast-iron-panties jokes.

I knew I needed to decide what type of girl I was going to become—a Shannon or a Rachel. Having been raised in a Christian home with a healthy dose of the abstinence philosophy, my standard had always been to keep myself pure for my future husband. But I wasn't sure how willing I was to keep that standard if it meant becoming totally unattractive—a turnoff, as Trevor would say—to every guy I met.

I started to ponder another option—keeping my virginity for my future husband, but going incognito as a girl who slept around. That way, I reasoned, I could keep my standard and still be desirable to the opposite sex.

For the next season of my life, I attempted to follow this brilliant plan. In my dating relationships, I developed the skill of going as far as I possibly could physically without "technically" having sex. And I consciously tried to communicate to everyone around me that I was definitely *not* one of those holier-than-thou, nunlike purity freaks.

I vividly remember a scene that took place in the frenzied hall at Ridgeview High School. I was engaged in the laborious process of shifting my impossibly heavy backpack to the other shoulder as I chatted with Derek Croitan and Beth Bridges, two brainy-yet-popular debate champions.

"You would not *believe* what Mr. Dixon said in his lecture today,"

Derek told us with an incredulous lip curl. Beth and I both looked at him with perked interest.

"He suggested that we have only *one* sexual partner for life, because monogamous people supposedly have less stress! Can you imagine actually doing that? Is that insane or what?" Derek laughed and shook his head in disbelief. Beth snorted and rolled her eyes in hearty agreement. I must have been quiet, because they both glanced over at me expectantly. I realized I had missed my cue.

"Oh, um, yeah," I quickly jumped in. "That is *so* ridiculous!"

Beth wasn't falling for it. She eyed me suspiciously. "Come on, Les, don't tell me you're one of those snooty uptight virgins who thinks you should be all pure until marriage or something!"

Derek's ears seemed to wiggle with anticipation while he awaited my reply. I could just hear him rushing off to his next class to inform all his buddies that he had just discovered a girl who was a total prude. I knew I could not let that happen.

"What*ever*," I argued confidently, scrunching up my face to display a defiantly disgusted expression. "Like I'm really all *pure* or something? Mr. Dixon would not want to know how many guys *I've* been with!"

Derek snickered and turned away, looking a little disappointed that he had not found a new subject for his famous uptight-virgin jokes after all. I trotted off to my next class, trying to act as flippant about the whole thing as possible, but inside I felt a sick knot form in my stomach. Somehow my plan had not worked very well. I was entrenched in a culture that mocked any desire within me to be pure. I had thought I could hold on to my standards in secret and at the same time fool my classmates into thinking I was the loose kind of girl they wanted me to be. But I couldn't fool my conscience. I was beginning to realize that I could not stand on both sides of the fence at the same time. And somehow I had ended up on the *wrong* side.

Something deep in my heart longed to go back to being the innocent girl I had once been, yet I knew I had already crossed over the line. Even though I might still be holding on to my technical virginity, there was really no true purity in my life at all. I had allowed the culture to convince me that it was worthless. I had worked so hard to be seen as someone with a complete disdain for purity that I had become just like the majority of the girls around me—carelessly discarding any remnant of lily whiteness that remained within my heart.

🦋 GROWING UP IN church, I had managed to grasp the concept of remaining physically pure for my future husband—a principle that I attempted, rather reluctantly, to live out in my life. Yet that was the extent of my understanding of purity. In my heart, there always lingered a secret longing to be lily white—to set aside my heart, mind, and body as untainted treasures that would one day be delicately cherished and highly valued by a gallant knight. But I had grown to be embarrassed by that inner desire.

The Christians in my life gave vague explanations of the benefits of purity, such as "Why eat a greasy hamburger now when you could have a world-class steak dinner later?" or "Christmas gifts are far more enjoyable and special if you don't open them early." (Weak arguments, in my opinion, since I liked greasy hamburgers far more than steak, and I thought presents were fun no matter *when* you opened them.) But they also informed me that this waiting thing was God's idea, and *that* logic was a little harder to argue with. Even though my church leaders communicated the importance of obeying God's law when it came to waiting, never once did they describe purity in the beautiful, dignified way I had always wanted it to be. Purity seemed like nothing more than a sterile rule—forced upon us for no apparent reason except to make us miserable while everyone else was having fun, or possibly so that we could one day find some distant benefit from living this way.

The other influences in my life—friends, guys, peers, Hollywood, and even teachers—usually had nothing but disgust and mockery for anything that resembled innocence. This was illustrated quite well by Trevor and Justin howling about Rachel's "cast-iron bras and panties" or Derek's scornful jokes about "snooty uptight virgins." To them, purity was something to be ridiculed and avoided, like a smelly, scab-encrusted vagrant. For years, I waffled between the two extremes. I tried to follow the rule of purity, not really knowing why, and at the same time show the world that I was like them—rejecting anything that smacked of set-apartness.

And then I encountered my true Prince, Jesus Christ. I looked deep into His gentle, noble eyes. Here was the gallant knight I had always hoped for, longed for, hardly dared to believe existed. My faded desire came rushing back with more intensity than I had ever known—I longed to be able to give Him the pure, untainted treasure of my heart, soul, mind, and body. I desperately wished I had kept myself set apart for Him—like a soft and pure white lily. But I knew that instead I was a trampled and tarnished thistle.

I couldn't stand the thought that I had ruined my chance to be set apart in purity for a heroic Prince who would cherish me. I couldn't bear to look at His perfect, dazzling, brilliant cleanness when I was covered with mud and dressed in filthy, tattered rags. But as I walked away, He followed me. I heard His soft whisper drifting over me, like the delicate breeze of spring.

"I can make you lily white," came His gentle voice. *"You can be set apart for Me. I can wash you clean, whiter than snow—if only you let Me."*

LILY WHITE? YEAH, RIGHT!

> *I have kicked myself off the throne of my life, so I no longer dictate how I live; but now Christ, living within me, has taken His position on my throne, and He determines how I live. This life I live in this earthly body, I now live in total dependence and trust in Jesus Christ who loved me and sacrificed everything for me.*
>
> GALATIANS 2:20, PARAPHRASE[3]

Just hearing the words *lily white* makes most of us want to grab our Nikes and head for the door with the speed of a runner charging onto the racetrack. There are plenty of reasons for this kind of sprinter reaction. Maybe we are one of the Mud Puddle Girls, who sigh resignedly, "I've been wallowing in this slimy mudhole for so long that I am hopelessly dirty—there is no way *I* can ever become lily white. It's too late for me, so why should I even try?"

Or perhaps we fall in line with the Comfort Club Ladies, who declare with a shrug, "My life is pretty good right now. I've got friends, popularity, romantic relationships, and Jesus is in there somewhere, too. Everything is going great. I'm just fine where I'm at—why would I want to rock the boat?"

Or we might relate to the Lazy Susans, who sleepily drawl, "*Lily* white? That's just a little *too* extreme, don't you think? I mean, I don't want to turn into one of those snobby, holier-than-thou types. I might consider a light cream color, or maybe even a soft eggshell hue, but let's not go overboard with this!"

And yet when we come face to face with our noble Prince, when we gaze into the depths of His tender eyes and feel His stirring voice within our souls, all those protests just disappear into nothingness, like the fleeting streak of a shooting star. True purity is so much more than a Christian rule to endure. True purity is so much more than the noble decision to wait for a future spouse. True purity is complete set-apartness for our heavenly Prince. True purity comes only when we fall into the loving arms of our Jesus Christ, surrender ourselves fully to Him, and allow Him to tenderly shape us into *His lily-white likeness.*

I mentioned earlier in this book that most of us think we know Christ. But very few of us really do. Those of us who grew up in Sunday school were trained from a young age that the right answer to nearly every question is "Jesus" and that if we memorized enough Bible verses, we would get a lollipop or a packet of shiny stickers. As we grew older, we learned how to impress the godly adults around us by saying, "Jesus is number one," or by wearing WWJD bracelets. We appeased our parents by going to youth group every week, listening to Christian music, going to Christian camps or on summer mission trips, and even cracking open our Bibles every now and then. Many of us went on to Christian universities or Bible colleges, and some of us even pursued careers in ministry. Even now, years later, we may be living moral lives full of integrity.

But how many of us truly *know* our Prince?

Maybe you didn't grow up in church but found Christianity later in life. Maybe you met Christ, allowed Him to become your Savior, cleaned up your life a little, and got plugged into a Christian group or church. Maybe you have great Christian friends, listen to inspiring Christian messages, sing passionate Christian songs, and even read lots of wonderful Christian books. Or maybe Christ is nothing more to you than an impersonal religious icon.

Are you ready to really *know* Him as your Prince?

Many of us know a lot *about* our Prince. But knowing *about* Him and *knowing* Him are two very different things. Do we *know* Jesus? Has He become the Lover of our souls, the essence of our very existence, the center of our entire beings, and the One for whom we would give up everything, including our very lives, to follow?

Knowing Him like *that* is not easy. In today's world (even the Christian world) we are usually living at an insanely frenzied pace of life, we are all too often bogged down with years of piled-up emotional baggage, we are distracted by confusing relationships or stressful circumstances, and we are bombarded by the relentless noise of the culture around us. The question is: how do we learn to know our Prince in the midst of all this? The answer is: *we can't.*

Jesus does not live at the frantic pace of this world. He is not found in the clanging clamor of the culture. His tender whisper is like a still, small voice that is quickly drowned out by our distracted minds and wandering hearts. To discover Him as our Prince, to *know* Him as our Lover—we must become like the princesses in our childhood fairy tales who were willing to leave *everything* else behind to follow the man each loved. We cannot stay where we are and go with our Prince.

🦌 OVER THE PAST several years—both via e-mail and in person—I have received "guy" questions from young women of all ages.

Jessica, a chipper, blue-eyed college sophomore from Pennsylvania, recently approached me with the question, "How can I keep being faithful to my future spouse when I have to sit there and watch all my friends have so much fun getting involved with guy after guy?"

Cassie, a twenty-one-year-old redhead, explained her dilemma to me in a sweet southern drawl: "There's a guy in my life who seems like he is everything I've been dreaming of in a husband—but right now we are just friends, and I have no idea how he feels about me. Should I talk to him about how I feel?"

Lisa, an intense first-year law student, wondered, "How do I stop feeling constant shame and guilt over all the mistakes I've made with guys in the past? And how do I find a guy who is interested in more than just using me?"

When I ask most young women if they have taken their perplexing issues to Christ, I usually get a very predictable answer: "Oh, yes, I've prayed and prayed about this. It's just that He hasn't given me any answers, and I really need to figure out what to do!"

Yet all too often, our "prayers" are nothing more than scattered sentences muttered in a hurry, whenever we happen to have a few spare seconds. The truth is, most of us as young women spend far more time and energy obsessing over guy issues than we do discovering our true Prince. In fact, many of us never even realize that an intimate knowledge of our Prince is even possible.

Instead, we spend our energy worrying about the "bigger" problems of life…like guys. Yes, guy issues are important and are definitely worth thinking about (we will be dealing with many of those issues later in this book). But here is the truth: *an ongoing, passionate romance with our true Prince is the foundation for success in every other area of life.* We so often try to solve life's most perplexing dilemmas without having that vital foundation. We don't know Christ. We don't spend time with Him. We don't understand His heart. As a result, we wallow about in confusion and frustration. We utter quick prayers here and there, and when we hear no reply from heaven, we assume it is up to us to figure out life on our own. Then we end up making terrible mistakes and wondering where He was the whole time. But there is so much more about our Prince to be discovered—an incredible, amazing love story just waiting to unfold.

If we are ready, the love story we have always dreamed of can begin right now. But not just any love story—the most beautiful, amazing, tender, perfect love story of all time…the romance between a bride and her Bridegroom. No matter who we are, what we have done, or how many mistakes we have made—our Prince is longing for us. He is ready to rescue us from our dungeons, transform us into His princesses, and gently shape us into His lily-white likeness for all the world to see.

When I finally surrendered my life to my Prince, I was struck for the first time with the incredible reality of what He had done for me. Growing up in Sunday school, I had limited my perception of Him to what I'd seen on the flannel board. When I was five, I had acknowledged that He died for my sins. But I had never fully grasped the awesome wonder of that truth. My Prince gave up His life to save me. It was the ultimate romantic gesture of all time. My destiny was an eternity of unspeakable suffering—an eternity without my Prince. There was no way I could ever hope to be with someone like Him—a pure, perfect, sinless, holy, righteous, majestic, sovereign, powerful King. I was nothing but a tainted, impure, sinful, unholy, wretched pauper. There was an impenetrable wall that separated me from my Hero—in His perfect and pure holiness, He could never dwell with me in my prison of sin.

And yet He saw me in the midst of my miserable, hopeless, filthy condition. He loved me and longed for me. There was only one way He could save me from my dungeon of eternal captivity—to purchase me with His very blood. He spilled out His life and died a horrible, agonizing death He did not deserve—all so that I could become His lily-white princess, His spotless bride for all of eternity. The moment He paid the price to purchase me, the wall between us came crashing down. He made the way, through the sacrifice of His own blood, for me to be with Him forever. His sacrifice was meant not just to keep me out of hell, but to make an ongoing, passionate, intimate love story with Him possible.

This is what my Prince did for me. And this is what *your* Prince did for *you*. He is the ultimate romantic, the most amazing hero, the perfect gentleman, the most powerful of all kings, and the most tender of all lovers. And He is waiting for you. Whether you have known Him most of your life but have allowed your intimacy with Him to grow stale, whether you have acknowledged Him as Savior but have never experienced a passionate romance with Him, or whether you have never met Him at all—if you are ready to know Him as your Prince, come to Him and tell Him so. Fall into His waiting arms and surrender your entire life to Him. Allow the reality of His love and sacrifice for you to penetrate your soul. He gave everything for you. Will you give everything to Him in return? The journey of a set-apart young woman starts here.

(If you are feeling unsure how to encounter Christ in an intimate way, rest assured we will spend much of the rest of this book discussing how to do that. For now, simply search your heart and ask Him to make you willing to know Him.)

CHAPTER THREE IN A NUTSHELL

Found within the antiquated folds of girlish fairy tales is the secret key to unlocking femininity. From Snow White to the Little Mermaid we discover: *behind every storybook princess is a noble and gallant prince.* But far beyond winsome tales of fictional romance is a breathtaking reality—the noble Hero of our long-lost girlish dreams is real! His name is Jesus. This Prince is not just your average Joe with baggy shorts and a patchy goatee. He is a man unlike all others, with a kiss of life on His lips and a castle far away. With a twinkle in His eyes, He calls us to "come away" with Him and become His princesses. He asks us to give up everything to be His bride. And the secret to unlocking the magnificent dimensions of our femininity, much like our fairy-tale princess counterparts, is found in our response: *to give up everything we possess to follow our gallant Knight.*

Our Prince is eager to begin a heavenly love story with us. He desires to spring from the pages of Scripture and dance with us in our real, day-to-day lives. He gave His very life on a cross for this opportunity to share life intimately at our sides. The defining question of our femininity is this: will we be willing to give our very lives to Him in return? He eagerly awaits our replies.

4

The Sacred Sanctuary

Creating the Inward Environment

What! Do you not realize that your body is a sacred sanctuary for
the Holy Spirit, the treasure of the heavenly Prince within,
and that your body belongs to Him and not you?

1 CORINTHIANS 6:19, PARAPHRASE[4]

I DISCOVERED MY Prince. I surren-
dered my life to Him. I declared that I was ready for our love story to
begin. He had taken my filthy rags and clothed me in the shining
white gown of a princess. I was His. But the journey had only just
begun.

Tenderly He whispered to my heart, *"You are a princess in title*
only. Now I want to teach you how to live *as My lily-white princess, how*
to live a life that is truly set apart for Me. There is so much more for you
to discover—there are boundless depths for you to explore!"

A LIFESTYLE OF LILY WHITENESS

There was a lot for me to learn about living the life of His lily-white princess. I had grown up right along with the throng of churched young adults who assumed that meeting Jesus Christ and living by a few basic morals was all there really was to the Christian life. Whenever I compared myself to the world around me—my non-Christian peers who slept with guy after guy, trashed their bodies with drugs and alcohol, lied to their parents constantly, and cheated their way through school—I felt as if I were truly living a set-apart life. But my standards were only slightly above the slimy sludge of the culture surrounding me. Purity was simply trying not to technically have sex before marriage. Standing up for Christ was merely refusing to smoke pot at a Friday-night party or showing up for group prayer at the school flagpole once a year. Living a godly life was nothing more than refusing to cheat on tests or get drunk, showing up for church once a week, and flipping through my Bible from time to time. The morals that governed my life were only rules I forced myself to obey in order to stay on Christ's "good side."

Christianity had become an enforced social club I was required to join. But it wasn't completely without benefits. It enabled me to hang around other people who were supposedly living by the same morals I had adopted so that I didn't feel so weird about being "different." It provided me with many fun-filled activities: I would scream and dance and sway at Christian concerts; I would flirt and laugh and bond at Christian retreats; I was able to discuss perplexing moral dilemmas in my Christian study groups; and I even got a few free, cool-looking, Christian T-shirts to add to my wardrobe. But my life on the inside was no different than that of the rest of the world: self-absorbed and stressed out, disillusioned and depressed, watered down and wounded, compromised and cowardly. My mind, heart, soul, thoughts, attitudes, habits, dreams, and desires were *nothing* like that of a lily-white princess.

When I encountered my true Prince in a new way, my perspective drastically changed. Suddenly, my sole longing was to know Him more, to understand Him more, and to grow closer and closer to Him. The life I had always lived seemed like a hollow, empty, meaningless existence in light of the spectacular beauty and majesty of my Prince. As I traveled with Him further and further away from the familiar dungeon walls, my heart began to overflow with more and more passionate love for Him. His words came back to me: *"You are a princess in title only."* I was filled with a passionate desire to be completely set apart for Him—not just to carry the title of being His princess, but to think, act, speak, and live like His princess every day of my life. Not just to be made clean *once,* but to live a lifestyle of lily whiteness for my Prince. I wasn't sure how to begin. But my heavenly Lover was ready and eager to show me. As soon as we arrived in His beautiful land, my "princess lessons" began.

"To live as My princess," He told me gently, *"I must become the center of your very existence. Your innermost being must become a set-apart place, a* sacred sanctuary *worthy of My presence. Your heart must be transformed into an intimate retreat, unstained by the pollution of the world, where you can discover more and more of Me and allow Me to shape you into My lily-white likeness."*

It was a vision that left me breathless with awe and eager with desire: to build a beautiful sacred sanctuary for my heroic Lord within my innermost being and discover the deepest intimacy with Him in that set-apart place. I was passionately excited to begin. My Prince gently warned me that the building of this sanctuary would not be easy.

"There are many things rooted within your heart that must first be

removed in order for a sacred sanctuary to be built there," He said with tender firmness, *"and the process will be painful."*

"I am ready," I told Him. And the building of my sacred sanctuary began. With the gentle guidance of my Hero, there were many practical steps I took in my life to create an inner sanctuary for Him. First, I had to cleanse and prepare the inner environment of my heart to house a sanctuary for Him. Next, I had to build my outward lifestyle around my newly created inner sanctuary.

If you have discovered your true Prince, if you are ready to leave behind everything else to go with Him, if you are willing to rise above the mediocre sludge of what passes for the typical Christian life, if you want your heavenly Lover to become the center of your very existence, if you are ready to become a set-apart young woman, a lily among thorns, the first step is to begin building a sacred inner sanctuary for your heavenly Lover. The building process is not an easy one, but finding endless depths of intimacy with Christ in this sacred place is the most breathtakingly beautiful experience you will ever know. The sacred sanctuary is where you will discover more and more of your Prince and where you will be transformed into His lily-white likeness. Your Prince is waiting to meet you there.

An Unforgettable Wedding Night

Imagine it is your wedding night. You are sitting in the backseat of the limo with your new husband, driving away from the church as your friends and family happily wave, tearfully blow kisses, and festively throw rice. The ceremony was perfect. Your handsome groom slipped the wedding ring on your finger and whispered his promise to love and cherish you forever. You are floating on a cloud of euphoria. The night you have always dreamed about has finally arrived! You look lovingly at your new husband, and he softly brushes his lips against yours. Your heart beats with excitement. You can't wait to share this night of tender intimacy with the man you love.

When the two of you finally arrive outside the bedroom door of your new home, your husband sweeps you into his arms and carries you across the threshold.

"I have dreamed of this moment my entire life," he whispers. "I love you so much!"

He tenderly sets you down. Your heart overflows with passionate love for your groom. It is going to be an unforgettable night of romance. But no sooner do your feet touch the floor than you begin to sense that something is wrong. Your husband notices it too. His face is bewildered as he looks slowly around the room. An intense, nauseating odor begins to surround you.

"What is that *smell*?" you ask, covering your nose in disgust. You flip on the nearest light switch and gasp in horror—there is *trash* everywhere! Piles and piles of garbage bags overflowing with slimy refuse lay scattered haphazardly throughout the room. Flies buzz around heaps of gooey, used pop cans and sticky banana peels. You stare at the sight in shocked revulsion. Is this someone's idea of a belated, bachelor-party joke?

But before you can speculate about which of your so-called friends is going to be in serious trouble for such a twisted attempt at humor, your attention is drawn to the far corner of the room. Some of your past boyfriends are casually leaning against the wall. One of them looks at you slyly. "Hey, babe," he says softly, his eyes full of charming seduction. He slowly walks toward you (stepping gingerly over a large Hefty bag of rotten grass clippings) and reaches out his hand to touch the side of your face.

You are speechless. This is supposed to be your wedding night—

a private, intimate, beautiful time between you and your new husband. It was meant to be the most romantic night of your life, and it is quickly turning into the most horrifying experience you ever could have imagined. You glance over at your groom. He is hanging his head mournfully and making his way dejectedly back down the hall.

"Wait!" you call out. "Where are you going?"

"I'm sorry," he says, shaking his head sadly, "I just can't be with you tonight—not like this." His face is overcome with agony and sorrow as he stumbles out the door. You chase after him in your wedding dress, which is now stained with a blob of spaghetti sauce that dripped out of one of the trash bags. But your groom is gone. Your wedding night has been completely and utterly ruined.

Okay, you can breathe a deep sigh of relief. It is highly unlikely that this scenario will happen to you on your wedding night! There is not a sane young woman on the planet who would allow heaps of slimy trash bags or sex-crazed former lovers to occupy her bedroom at *any* time, let alone during a romantic night with the man of her dreams. And yet when it comes to intimacy with Jesus Christ, so many of us do just that. We pray for more intimacy with Him, ask Him to join us in the innermost part of our being, but we fail to realize there is so much garbage in the way that He can hardly get through the door. We wonder how to "fall in love with Jesus Christ," yet we conveniently forget about the scores of other lovers who have staked their claims on the territory of our hearts and constantly draw our attention and affection away from our true Prince.

Building a sacred inner sanctuary for intimacy with our Prince is a lot like creating a private, romantic retreat for intimacy between a husband and wife. Clean, fresh, romantic surroundings are crucial to intimacy between lovers. Things like flowers, candles, and soft music set the stage for an unforgettable night. Piles of disgusting garbage spread around the bedroom or former lovers standing in the corner, trying to seduce you, will rapidly annihilate any spark of intimacy between a man and woman! In the same way, deep and tender intimacy with our heroic Lord is impossible while heaps of sin, emotional garbage, and other lovers occupy our hearts.

Taking Out the Trash

> *Christ's set-apart ones have all gone through the same inner-transformation process. They have all kicked Self off the throne of their lives, eliminating the controlling power of sin, and offered the heavenly Prince the ruling power of their existence.*
>
> Galatians 5:24, paraphrase[5]

More than likely, most of our "trash" has been residing within us for so long we don't even realize it's there. And yet its presence will hinder true intimacy with our Lord for as long as it is allowed to remain in our hearts. A lifestyle of lily whiteness can flow only out of an inner being that has been made lily white by Jesus Christ.

The garbage lingering in your soul can be anything from that seemingly small lie you told when you were eight, to deep-seated hatred toward someone who abused you, to ongoing compromises you allow in your life on a regular basis, to a horrible memory from your past, unresolved and locked tightly within the caverns of your heart. Whatever junk resides within you, your Prince is ready and waiting to remove it from you completely—as far away as the east is from the west (see Psalm 103:12).

It is so easy to feel that it is too late, that somehow you have crossed the line and are beyond His forgiveness and cleansing power. But this is the very reason He sacrificed His life for you—so that He could wash you clean and make you into His lily-white princess forever. If you are willing to offer every piece of your heart to your Prince for Him to cleanse and renew, you will not be disappointed.

When I realized how much my Prince desired intimacy with me in my inner sanctuary, I was determined to remove any hindrance or distraction that might stand in the way. One night, when I knew I had plenty of uninterrupted time, I shut myself in my room and prepared to do some deep internal cleansing. It would have been so much easier to just say a simple blanket prayer, asking God to forgive all the sins I had ever committed. But to prepare the environment of my heart to house a sacred sanctuary for Him, there was more that needed to be done. The effects of the sinful lifestyle I had lived were cluttering up every corner of my inner being. I had deep emotional scars, secret memories locked up within me, and very *un*-lily-white habits that controlled my actions and attitudes every single day. It was time for some serious trash removal.

With a pen and notebook in my hand and songs of surrender playing softly in the background, I knelt and asked God to show me, one by one, every past or present sin in my life that needed to be dealt with. Memories came to my attention that had long been forgotten; part of me wished they could stay that way. But gradually, as I dealt with each pile of sinful trash that lay scattered within my heart, I began to feel a freedom unlike any I'd ever known. The process was awkward and painful. I sat down with my parents and tearfully repented of the lies I had told them and the hundreds of ways I had shown them disrespect. I called friends and asked their forgiveness for gossiping, lying, backstabbing, selfishness—and the list went on. I apologized to my younger brothers for not being a Christlike example to them.

I determined to make things right in every area of my heart and life to the best of my ability. I destroyed remnants of damaging past relationships that still had a hold over my heart—notes from former flings, photos of past boyfriends, even some of my old yearbooks that carried the weight of some serious emotional baggage with them. I asked my Prince to come in and occupy every piece of my heart that had been taken over by past romantic relationships.

I threw away seductive outfits that I had bought for no other purpose than to draw the attention of guys. I tossed stacks of popular magazines that were fun to read but had subtly filled my mind with a disdain for innocence. I got rid of music that applauded impurity. It did not matter how small or subtle the compromise seemed; if there was even a hint of impurity in it, I snuffed it out of my life. This cleansing process had nothing to do with following spiritual "rules," or trying to "appease" Christ by being as perfect as possible—it was something I did naturally and willingly, out of a heart overflowing with love and desire for Him. I wanted absolutely *nothing* to stand in the way of discovering true intimacy with my heavenly Lover.

This process of taking the trash out of my heart was worth every bit of pain and discomfort it caused me. Years of garbage had been residing within my inner being, destroying all chances of intimacy with Christ. When He removed sin's claim over my soul and washed my inner being lily white, He became the sole occupant of every corner of my heart. I still struggled with sinful tendencies, but whenever any old trash tried to creep back in, I was much more aware of its presence and much quicker to get rid of it.

Regular trash removal became a vital, ongoing process in my life from that point forward. And each time I allowed myself to receive Christ's cleansing touch, as painful as it might be, it chased me even deeper into the loving, healing embrace of my heroic Lord.

PRACTICAL STEPS FOR TAKING OUT THE TRASH

To prepare our inward environment for intimacy with our Prince, it is important to walk through a focused process of trash removal.

It is wise to set aside a long period of time when interruptions are unlikely. It is often necessary to unplug the phone and turn off the computer, or find a secluded spot outdoors. As you prepare for the trash removal process, clear your mind of any potential distractions and make a focused decision to concentrate on nothing else but the internal cleansing process. Invite your Prince to thoroughly examine every nook and cranny of your heart. With pen and paper ready, ask Him to show you any hidden sins lingering within you, any subtle compromises or wrong habits you have allowed to creep into your life, and any situation or relationship in your life that needs to be made right.

For this process, I highly recommend taking some time to work through part 1 of the material entitled "Inner Sanctuary," available at www.authenticgirl.com. This material is extremely detailed and very similar to the guidelines I used during my own internal cleansing process. Though everyone's "trash-removal" process is different, this material can help serve as a catalyst for God's unique work in your own heart.

Whatever our Prince asks you to do, don't wait another moment before obeying. The longer you put it off, the easier it is to justify it away, and the quicker you end up right back where you started—in a smelly, trash-infested house with a spaghetti-sauce-stained wedding dress and a tear-stained groom. Your Prince is longing for intimacy with you. He is longing to help you build your inner sanctuary. No matter what you have done in your life and no matter what has been done to you, nothing is beyond His eternal cleansing power. He, and He alone, can wash you clean and make you lily white.

KICKING OUT OTHER LOVERS

> *To be my disciple, to be a set-apart one, costs every-thing you have. Don't delude yourself into thinking it will only cost you a portion of your existence! The very essence of a disciple is one who has completely emptied her inner sanctuary of all other lovers to make room for Me, her heavenly Prince.*
>
> LUKE 14:33, PARAPHRASE[6]

The very thought of my first serious crush (remember Brandon, the Vanilla Ice look-alike?) joining Eric and me on our wedding night is enough to send me into a state of intense nausea. The deep love and commitment I share with Eric is in an altogether different strato-sphere from the meaningless emotional flings I experienced with past boyfriends. Eric and I have built our marriage upon implicit trust and commitment-based intimacy. Nothing would kill our intimacy faster than the thought of other lovers being in the picture. If Eric did not know without question that he is the only man in my life, he would never be able to fully offer his heart to me. Our relationship would be strained with tension and distrust. Deep, trusting, tender, loving inti-macy between us would be impossible.

In the same way, intimacy with my Prince in a set-apart inner sanctuary was impossible as long as other lovers lingered within the corners of my heart. I recalled the tender words of my Hero: *"I must become the center of your very existence."* My entire heart needed to become His alone. My worshipful adoration must belong to Him alone—to nothing and to no one but my true Prince. I had been secretly clinging to many things, things that possessed an unhealthy hold over my heart, mind, and affections. They were things that stood in the way of complete and unhindered devotion to my Lord. Once again, I set aside a focused period of time to ask Christ to show me all the other lovers hiding in my heart. As He gently pointed to one after another, I was amazed at how much of my time, thoughts, energy, and devotion were constantly being given to things other than Him. The list was long: from my obsessive need to pursue people's approval, to my driving desire to find security through romantic relationships, to my longing to be successful at everything I attempted. These were the areas I spent most of my time and energy pursuing. These were the things I was devoted to. These were the things I worshiped. Now I knew I must loosen my death grip on them, open my hands, and throw them to the wind so that I could spend my time and energy pursuing my Prince instead. I needed to devote myself to Him alone, find my security in Him alone, and worship Him alone.

The process of kicking out these other lovers was even more painful than the trash removal had been. One by one, I showed them to the door. I began saying no to the frenzied social activities that had been the center of my life and helped me climb the popularity ladder. I started avoiding the usual hookup spots that had allowed me to be noticed by potential romantic flings. I relinquished my carefully planned future goals and told my Prince He could do anything He wanted to do with my life and future.

As I stepped off the fast track of popularity and success, I felt as if I was being stripped of everything that had given me confidence for years. Questions and fears plagued my mind. *If I don't chase after romantic relationships, won't I always be lonely and insecure? If I don't pursue popularity, won't I become one of those strange social recluses who lives in the woods and has no friends? If I don't build my life around success and achievements, what will become of my future?*

"Am I enough?" came the gentle challenge of my Prince, and His tender voice drowned out all the clamoring confusion in my mind. Jesus was, and would always be, much more than enough. He did not desire to destroy my life, to leave me as a desolate, lonely failure alone in the woods somewhere. He gently assured me that as I pursued Him and Him alone, all my other needs would be met. In the meantime, my only concern must be to worship Him with everything in me.

PRACTICAL STEPS FOR KICKING OUT OTHER LOVERS

> *Delight yourself in the LORD;*
> *and He will give you the desires of your heart.*
>
> PSALM 37:4

This is one of my favorite verses. It illustrates the loving faithfulness of our Lord. As we dwell on Jesus Christ, He fills our hearts with *His* desires for our lives, and we are completely fulfilled by *Him.* And yet, most of us have it backward. We aggressively try to meet the desires of our hearts by pursuing romantic relationships, popularity, comfort, material possessions, or achievements instead of truly delighting in Jesus Christ.

And yet even God-given desires can gain an unhealthy hold over our hearts and lives, such as the longing to finally experience a beautiful, God-written love story with one person for a lifetime. As precious as this dream is, it is all too easy to make this desire the focus of our lives. As a result, we miss out on experiencing the most beautiful love story of all time with our true Prince. The reality is that the only way to discover the true beauty of a God-written love story with another person on this earth is to delight in Jesus Christ with all our heart, soul, mind, and strength—to find our security and joy in Him alone. Rather than focus all our efforts on the pursuit of a human relationship, we must center our lives on the *pursuit of intimacy with our true Prince.* Only out of intimacy with our heavenly Lover can the beauty of a God-written human love story be experienced.

To prepare the environment of our inner sanctuary for intimacies with our Prince, any other lovers—anything we devote a huge part of our time, emotion, energy, and affection to—must be ushered to the door and kicked out. That means anything that has an unhealthy hold over our hearts and compromises our ability to be completely devoted to Christ. Often these are the things that we derive most of our earthly confidence, security, and happiness from. They are the things we cling to most tightly, the things we can't imagine giving up or living without.

Much like the previous process of taking out the trash, removing these other lovers can be a difficult task. It is a wise idea to set aside a focused period of time for this process. Again, I highly recommend taking some time to work through part 2 of the material entitled "Inner Sanctuary," available at www.authenticgirl.com.

As your Prince brings to mind the other lovers that possess a strong hold over your heart, remember that often it is not enough to simply acknowledge that He is more important to you than those things. Most likely, practical changes must be made in your life so that you can devote your time, energy, thoughts, and affections to Him alone. If you have been obsessed with being noticed by the opposite sex, it may be time to avoid the places you normally go for that purpose. If you are overly attached to some musician or band, you might need to consider getting rid of those posters and albums. If you are in a romantic relationship that is taking precedence over your relationship with Jesus Christ, you might need to take a step away from that relationship to refocus your life around Him.

It can be excruciatingly painful to get rid of the other lovers we have been clinging to. But once they are gone and we are able to enjoy unhindered intimacy with our Prince, we will never wonder if it was worth it. He is enough—*so much more* than enough. All of my fears about living as an isolated, lonely hermit in the woods disappeared when I experienced true, unhindered intimacy with Him. The other areas of my life were not destroyed, but only *enhanced* through my relationship with my Prince.

"Delight yourself in the LORD; and He will give you the desires of your heart." Instead of trying to satisfy the desires of our hearts through meaningless pursuits, we must *delight ourselves completely in the amazing love of our true Prince*—as we focus on Him, we will be more than fulfilled.

CHAPTER FOUR IN A NUTSHELL

The deepest, most precious expressions of intimacy are not meant for crowded subways and busy supermarkets. Love notes are not read out loud in crowded bars, and love songs are not sung at garbage dumps. Intimacy with a lover is saved for sacred, set-apart places—places of aloneness and places that reflect the sweetness of the expressions of one's heart.

Intimacy with the Inventor of romantic love is no different. Our Prince longs to meet with us in the sacred environs of our hearts, alone, surrounded by the sweet fragrance of our mutual affection for each other. But for this to happen, we must each prepare for Him an intimate and sacred sanctuary, a quiet and beautiful place adorned with His light and set apart for His enjoyment alone.

It is in this holy chamber where we experience the life-altering closeness of our Prince and are transformed into more than princesses in title alone, but into princesses in behavior as well. It is in this heavenly haven that we learn to live like princesses in the way we think, feel, speak, walk, and talk. The set-apart life of a Christlike princess begins with the preparation of this sacred place. But the preparation of this sacred sanctuary is merely the beginning of the set-apart adventure. For in due time, a set-apart young woman discovers that this intimate place holds the divine secrets to an outrageously abundant and joy-filled life—a life of the most fulfilling intimacy with her Prince.

5

Beautiful Reflection

Shaping the Outward Lifestyle

*I eagerly give up all my prized possessions, I unhesitatingly forgo
the pleasure of my most intimate friendships, and,
without reservation, I void all my greatest achievements
for the amazing and priceless opportunity to intimately know,
love, and serve my heavenly Prince, Jesus Christ.*

PAUL THE APOSTLE, PHILIPPIANS 3:8, PARAPHRASE[7]

MY INNER SANCTUARY was
beginning to take shape. I had carefully cleaned out the years of piled-
up garbage that had cluttered my inner being. I had ruthlessly
removed the other lovers that had occupied the corners of my heart.
I was ready to discover beautiful and unhindered intimacy with my
Prince. But there was still another crucial element to the building of
my inner sanctuary.

"*Stop trying to fit Me into your life; instead,* build your life around
Me," came the gentle request of my heroic Lord.

69

The typical chaos of my daily life was leaving very little room left over for true intimacy with my Prince.

LOOKING BEYOND ASSUMPTIONS

The pattern of frenzy had started in high school. From the first week of my freshman year, I had adopted the lifestyle of the typical American teen. My daily routine had always been the same. My alarm clock would go off at precisely 6:00 a.m. with a hideous shriek, as if it took some secret delight in rudely shocking me out of my comfortable dream world every morning. Groggily, I would stumble out of bed and into the bathroom and immediately flip on my radio to the crude and meaningless banter of Josh and Bo—the two popular local disc jockeys on the *Wake Up and Get Crazy Morning Show*. I would get ready for school in a sleep-deprived stupor, then race downstairs just in time to grab a bagel, shoving it in my mouth as I rushed out the door to squish into the backseat of Molly Clark's red Mustang convertible. On the insanely jerky drive to school, as Molly ignored nearly every traffic law ever written, I would eagerly dive right into the usual shallow gossipy chatter with my friends—sneering with haughty disdain about Jennifer Cathcart's despicably tacky homecoming dress, or reveling in the fact that the gorgeous Joey Jenkins had just dumped the incredibly snobby Chelsea Watson after only two weeks.

Once I arrived at school, my friends and I would lounge on tables in the cafeteria, nibbling on candy or slurping pop (eating junk food before 8:00 a.m. somehow made us cooler), scribbling on last-minute homework assignments, and flirting playfully with any cute guy who happened to be hanging around. Then (strangely reminiscent of my irritating morning alarm clock) the overhead bell would passionately squawk. I would race off to start my school day, where I sat like a zombie through lecture after lecture, trying to force my distracted mind to grasp at least some small amount of academic knowledge.

After school I would rush home and inhale some highly nutritious snack (usually SpaghettiOs or Kraft Macaroni & Cheese) as I vegged on the couch in front of a mindless sitcom. Then I would head to my room, crank up the stereo, and plop down on my bed with my homework and, more important, the phone. I would alternate between halfhearted study and meaningless phone chats for a couple of hours. Then I was off to one of my many nightly activities: youth group, study group, cheerleading, choir rehearsal, drama rehearsal, voice lessons, piano lessons—the list went on. I would usually crash into bed by midnight and then start the routine all over again the next day.

On the weekends, I devoted all my time to catching up on sleep and maintaining my demanding social life. I crammed every spare moment with parties, movies, concerts, football games, dates, youth group get-togethers, and shopping with friends. This was the normal, healthy, expected life of a girl my age. I had never questioned it. The fact that I was involved in so many activities and constantly surrounded with friends had always been my "great Christian witness"— proving to the world that just because a young person was a Christian did not mean that he or she couldn't survive on the fast track of the typical American teen.

This crazy pace of life only seemed to continue, in different forms, the older I got. Friends, guys, and career pursuits completely dominated my time. I had been trying to fit Him in here and there, whenever I had a spare moment. Though a lot of my time was spent with Christian friends doing Christian things, He was not the center of my world. My life was not built around my Prince. What had been the point of preparing my heart for intimacy with Him if I never had time to meet Him in my inner sanctuary?

And yet I had no idea how to build my life around Him. At first glance, there seemed to be hardly anything that I could cut out. Abandon my friends? Withdraw from my activities? Skip out on my school and career goals? Shut down my dating life altogether? How could I make decisions like this and expect to live a normal existence? Patiently, my Prince opened my eyes to a new understanding: as His lily-white princess, I should not expect to live a "normal" existence ever again. He had so much more in mind for me than the expected pattern for today's typical young woman. And He wanted to teach me to think outside the assumptions I had never questioned—assumptions that controlled the way I lived my daily life.

ASSUMPTION #1: *To be well adjusted and healthy, a young woman must have plenty of friends her own age and must spend a large amount of her time and energy maintaining those friendships.*

Even after I made the decision to stop chasing after popularity, I still found myself feeling the need to maintain at least a decent number of friendships. Yet when I stepped back and really examined those friendships, I was surprised to realize that the majority of my friends were not *true* friends. They did not really *know* me, nor did they have a desire to. I was simply another voice in the midst of their gossipy chatter, another body squished in the backseats of their cars, another ear for their jokes and secrets, another workout partner, or another shopping buddy. Though many of them were so-called Christians, they did not have the remotest understanding of my desire to pursue intimacy with my Prince. If I were to try to explain it to them, I would be met only by blank stares. Why did I feel the need to devote my time to maintaining these shallow relationships?

I discovered that my reasons were based around the assumption that if I did not have plenty of friends my own age, I would not be normal and healthy. I would be isolated and alone. I would be strange. I would forget how to relate to society. I would be on my way to that remote and depressing hermit's cabin in the woods. But the gentle voice of my Prince, drawing me toward intimacy with Him, began to challenge this ingrained assumption. Wasn't *He* far more important to me than being considered normal? Even if it meant that I never had friends again and became a social outcast, with all my heart I wanted to build my life around Him. So I withdrew from my circle of friends. They hardly noticed I was gone. Surprisingly, I found that I did not miss them either.

My Lord was amazingly faithful to meet my needs for human companionship by bringing *true* friends into my life—friends who were pursuing Him in the same way I was. They were friends who understood my commitment to building my life around Christ, and I did not have to spend huge amounts of my time or energy maintaining the friendships. They were not always friends my own age. Some of them, shockingly enough, were actually right in my own family. Others were godly adults in my life, much older and wiser than me. They were people who I never would have thought of as potential friends. They were not typically the "normal" friends a young woman today is expected to have. But they were the most supportive, encouraging, like-minded companions I had ever known. They led me closer to my Jesus Christ. They helped pave the way for intimacy with Him in my inner sanctuary.

ASSUMPTION #2: *To have a successful future, a young woman must carefully follow society's pattern for success.*

The seeds for this assumption were planted at an early age. My first week of high school, I had been forced—along with the rest of my fellow ninth-grade inmates—to sit through a lecture entitled "Freshman Seminar." During this enlightening experience, Mr. Armstrong (a bulky JV football coach and part-time guidance counselor) attempted to scare us into taking our education seriously by explaining the ABCs of academic reality for today's young American adult.

"I know you all think you're here to meet friends and have a good time," he began in a deadly serious voice, tightening his jaw for added effect, "but that's not what high school is about. People, you have got to *wake up!*" His voice raised a couple of decibels with those last two words, and he started pacing back and forth in agitation as he continued his passionate speech. I never forgot Mr. Armstrong's words that day.

"Do you know what happens to people who don't get into a good college?" he boomed, gazing at us with narrowed eyes. When no one ventured a guess, he exploded with the answer: "They end up working their fingers bloody on fifteen-hour shifts at the toothpaste factory! They make $1.50 an hour! They have no money for their families and end up living off welfare. Pretty soon, the factory cuts back and they get laid off. They have nowhere else to go but the homeless shelter! You think *they* have time to party? You think *they* have time for fun?" Mr. Armstrong's face was red, and he was practically screaming. In the back of my mind, I vaguely wondered if his facts weren't just a little exaggerated, but he was so convincing that he quickly won my full attention.

Mr. Armstrong went on to inform us of the sobering requirements for getting into a good college. We stared at him with wide eyes as he raised his husky arms in the air and emphatically warned us that if we did not maintain a decent GPA throughout high school—especially our freshman year, which was extremely crucial to the whole plan—we had no prayer of being accepted into a good college, we would never amount to anything, and we were headed straight for the homeless shelter. I went home that night, armed with a huge pile of college brochures that had been passed out at the end of Mr. Armstrong's lecture, and carefully laid out my ten-year plan.

From that young age, the way to do things had been ingrained in my mind, and I had never questioned society's pattern for success:

make top grades in high school, be career-minded from the age of fourteen, get into a good college, graduate with honors, find a high-paying job, make a lot of money, buy a nice car and big house, and, most of all, steer clear of ending up in a homeless shelter! I became goal-oriented and ambitious, and I was committed to living the American dream.

But my Lord had something far better in mind for me. *"Can you trust Me with your future?"* He whispered. Mr. Armstrong's threats from my freshman year came racing back into my mind. If I let my Prince have full reign over the direction of my life, my carefully laid ten-year plan might be compromised. Irrational worries that had been planted years ago began to haunt me. What if I ended up in the toothpaste factory and then the homeless shelter? The culture had trained me well—fears of what would become of me viciously attacked my mind. But the patient whisper of my Prince continued to tug at my heart. Finally one day I was ready to allow Him full access to my future plans—to do with my life whatever He desired.

The most important focus of my life shifted to building my daily existence around intimacy with Him in my inner sanctuary. I realized it was nearly impossible to do this with my current schedule, so, with plenty of fear and trembling but also with plenty of support from my parents, I made the decision to finish my high-school education at home. I was amazed at what happened as a result of that choice. Every day, before doing anything else, I was able to spend a long, focused period of time alone with my Prince. For the first time in my life, things that pulled me away from Him did not assault me throughout the day. The noise and distraction I had been so used to every day had disappeared. I began to hear His gentle voice even more clearly. I was able to build my life around Him.

Whenever a decision needed to be made about my future, instead of following the culture's push toward money and success, I began to allow Christ to lead me wherever *He* wanted me to go. As I made my Lord the center of my days, I quickly found that my obedience to His voice did not destroy my education, career, or future, but only enhanced those areas beyond my greatest imagination.

(A note if you are currently in high school: not every high schooler has the opportunity to finish school at home, and it might not even be God's best for you, although it is certainly worth considering and praying about if you do have that option. I encourage you, no matter what your situation, to think through what opportunities you *do* have to make different choices about the way you spend your time and energy—and be aware that Christ might be calling you to make some dramatic changes that feel uncomfortable at first.)

ASSUMPTION #3: *To find true love, a young woman must put a huge amount of effort into the pursuit of romantic relationships.*

Discovering my true Prince had more than satisfied my lifelong childhood desire to become the princess of a noble knight who would cherish me forever. But I still felt an unwavering pressure from the world around me to hurry up and "find that special someone" to spend the rest of my life with. I still desired to get married and have a family someday, and conventional wisdom told me that the longer I waited to snag someone, the less chance I had of seeing that desire fulfilled. My parents had been high-school sweethearts; they met at a dance when they were fifteen (back in the days when everything had a black-and-white *Leave It to Beaver* flair). This, along with the sage advice of the other young women I talked to, pushed me to start searching aggressively for the right guy, desperately hoping to find him before I missed my chance. I became convinced that if I hadn't found him by the time I graduated from college, I was doomed to be stuck having to choose from the "bottom of the pile," like arriving at the tail end of a huge half-off sale and finding nothing left but random, useless articles of clothing that don't fit.

Everything my Prince had challenged me to do recently—avoiding the usual places I went to meet and flirt with guys, finishing my education at home, and letting go of most of my social activities to focus more on Him—took me out of the dating scene. I began to worry that if I was not out there, I would never meet someone. Visions of that lonely hermit's cabin in the woods began to haunt me once again.

"Trust Me with your love story," came His tender voice. *"Allow Me to write each chapter of your future in My own perfect time and My own perfect way."*

Handing the pen of my love story over to my Prince was by far the most difficult step He ever asked me to take. Though He had never been anything but faithful in all other areas, still I was plagued by the fear that *this* area would be ruined if it were out of my control. Surely He needed the aid of my romantic expertise! What about that popular saying "God can't steer a parked car"? Didn't I need to rev up the engine for Him—get out there and make myself available to the opposite sex—and then keep a helping hand on the steering wheel as He drove in order to make sure He didn't crash the car?

"Trust Me, Leslie. Trust Me with all your heart; don't lean on your own understanding." The message He spoke to my heart could not have been clearer. He wanted me to stop building my life around the pursuit of the opposite sex and instead build my life completely around the pursuit of Him. I was to concern myself not with finding human love but with falling more deeply in love with Jesus Christ. In His own perfect way, when He was ready, He would write my love story for me.

If you have read previous books that Eric and I have written,[8] you already know the ending to this little drama. As I put the pen in the hands of my Prince (the *true* Author of romance) and focused my life completely on Him, He was amazingly faithful. In His own perfect time, He wrote a love story for me more beautiful than anything I could have ever dreamed. But it all began with a different, and much more important, love story—a passionate romance with my heavenly Lover and deep, devoted, unhindered intimacy with Him in the inner sanctuary of my heart.

PRACTICAL STEPS FOR PURSUING INTIMACY WITH CHRIST

Take a good long look at your relationship with your Prince. Have you built your entire life around pursuing intimacy with Him in the inner sanctuary of your heart? Or are you merely trying to fit Him into your life whenever it is convenient? It is easy to assume that just because your life is filled with Christian activities, Christian friends, Christian music, and Christian books, you are building it around Christ.

A young figure skater with the dream of winning an Olympic gold medal does not just read about skating, watch videos about skating, sing songs about skating, listen to advice about skating, and hang out with other skaters. She devotes her *heart, soul, mind, body, energy,* and *time* to skating. She gets up before dawn, practices tirelessly for countless hours, and spends every spare moment of her days, nights, and weekends on the ice. That kind of passionate, unyielding dedication is a picture of what it means to build our lives around intimacy with our Prince in the inner sanctuary of our hearts. Don't settle for hearing about intimacy with Him, singing about intimacy with Him, or reading about intimacy with Him; really *discover* true intimacy with Him by *building your entire life around Him.* A life built around our Prince is the essence of what it means to be His lily-white princess.

It is very likely that in order to build your life around Him there are practical, and often painful, changes that must be made to your life. For me, it meant letting go of several friendships, withdrawing from many activities, stopping the pursuit of the opposite sex, relinquishing my ten-year plan for education and career, and finishing my education in an unorthodox manner. The choices I made are by no means a formula that works for everyone; your own practical steps may be very different. Your practical changes could be anything from waking up earlier, to turning off the television, to stepping away from an all-consuming relationship or pursuit. It is important to realize that the reason for making practical changes in our lives is not because a certain activity, relationship, or pursuit is necessarily wrong, but because it is hindering us from building our entire lives around intimacy with our true Prince. As we will discuss throughout this book, a life built around intimacy with Him does not usually mean sitting in our rooms with Bibles in our laps 24/7! There is so much more to be discovered and explored when it comes to intimacy with our Prince.

Begin with the foundations of your life. Ask yourself these questions: *What are the things that consume my time, energy, and attention throughout the week? In what practical ways could I restructure my life to center around intimacy with my heavenly Lover?* With an open heart and mind, ask Him to show you what aspects of your life are hindering your ability to focus completely on Him. With His gentle guidance, do whatever it takes to build your life around Him. It will not be easy—but soon you will discover a depth of intimacy with your Prince you never knew was possible.

A Picture of Set-Apartness
SCOTLAND, 1889

Bright-eyed seventeen-year-old Amy walked through the damp streets, surrounded by her family and neighbors. It was an overcast Sunday morning. The weekly community church service had just ended. As the group moved along, talking politely to one another about the weather and the minister's sermon, there seemed to be nothing out of the ordinary about the familiar routine. But suddenly Amy's eye was drawn to a tattered old woman in rags, struggling under a heavy bundle as she moved sluggishly down the sidewalk. It was something never before seen in Amy's respectable neighborhood—a raggedy homeless woman making her way down the well-groomed streets, plodding past the dignified women in their expensive dresses and the cultured men in their tailored suits. The church people began to glance disapprovingly at the unsightly woman. She lumbered along painfully, bent over from the strain of the huge load she carried. A few people coughed nervously; others looked away in awkward silence.

In a spontaneous burst of compassion, Amy went to the old woman. Two of her brothers followed her lead. Together the three of them lifted the bundle from the woman's back and took her by the arms. They helped her continue down the street, moving slowly past dozens of fellow churchgoers, who watched the scene with disgruntled surprise. Amy's cheeks began to flush with embarrassment, and she instantly regretted her hasty decision to help the woman. As people continued to stare and frown, she felt her humiliation grow. What had she been thinking? To do such a thing in *this* neighborhood, among *these* people was unheard-of in Amy's day. Her foolish action would likely be gossiped about and criticized for weeks. A cold wind started to blow, and soon she and her brothers were covered with a mess of the old woman's tattered clothing, which only added to Amy's misery. She felt crimson all over. She resented the old woman, and her mind became preoccupied with what everyone was thinking of her.

But as the little group stumbled past a nearby fountain, Amy heard a voice flash through the gray fog, *"There is only one foundation worth building on—Jesus Christ."* Startled, she turned to see who had spoken, but everything was the same as it had been moments ago. No one around her seemed to have heard the voice. Amy began to feel a pull on her heart. She knew her Lord was speaking to her.

That afternoon she shut herself in her room to sort out her life's values. And from then on, her perspective was forever altered. [9] "Nothing could ever matter to me again," she wrote later, "but the things that were eternal."[10] Amy's love story with her Prince began that day, and she was transformed from an ordinary Christian girl into a lily among thorns—a set-apart young woman.

"The preoccupations of seventeen-year-old girls—their looks, their clothes, their social life—do not change much from generation to generation. But in every generation there seem to be a few who make other choices. Amy was one of the few," wrote Elisabeth Elliot in her biography of Amy Carmichael's life.[11]

To live a life set apart for her Prince, Amy had to make difficult choices. She made a decision to become "dead to the world and its applause, to all its customs, fashions, and laws."[12] No longer did she concern herself with what other people thought—she lived only for the smile of her Prince. No longer did she pour her energy into perfecting her wardrobe, appearance, and social life—she poured herself into knowing her Prince. No longer did she live out society's expected pattern for a young woman in that day—her life's ambition was to please her Prince alone. And her life became an incredible reflection of Him.

By the age of nineteen, Amy had a flourishing ministry to hundreds of poor factory girls in her community. The spunky young woman single-handedly raised the money to build a huge auditorium to hold Christian meetings specifically for the girls. On opening night, it was filled to capacity with over five hundred young women desperately in need of hope. As a local pastor began the ceremony to dedicate the building to Christ, Amy did not take her expected position of honor on the stage with the other leaders but sat quietly out of notice in the middle of the audience. She did not care about getting the credit she deserved for her hard work; her only concern was that Jesus Christ was the primary focus of everyone's attention.[13]

In her twenties, Amy said good-bye to her family, friends, and familiar life and bravely sailed across the ocean to offer her life as a missionary for her Prince. She went to India, where she began a dangerous effort to rescue hundreds of babies and children who were being sold into temple prostitution. Amy created a beautiful haven for those little ones to grow up in a Christ-centered environment. That unprecedented ministry—which began with only one devoted young woman—saved the lives of many precious children, brought many more to Christ, and still continues to this day. Amy wrote more than thirteen books that have impacted thousands of lives. Throughout her life, Amy lived a lifestyle of lily whiteness, motivated by her passionate love for her Prince. She sought to honor Him with every aspect of her existence, and many times it cost her dearly. Her life was an incredible, rare picture of set-apartness, the kind of life that has inspired countless people to truly discover Jesus Christ.

Amy's set-apart, world-altering existence started on that cold morning in Scotland when she was seventeen. She heard the voice of her Prince calling her to come away with Him. When Amy opened her heart to that call, nothing was ever the same again.

Today, examples of set-apart young women like Amy are hard to find. Even the Christian young women in today's culture are typically preoccupied with *anything but* their true Prince. And yet, as was said of Amy, in every generation there seem to be a few young women who make another choice—a choice to follow their Prince into the boundless depths of a set-apart existence. Are you willing to be one of the few?

CHAPTER FIVE IN A NUTSHELL

We each have a dream—something we build our lives around, something that gives us a spark of energy in our day-to-day existence. If our dream is ballet, we envision ourselves on stage elegantly dancing like a radiant cherub before an awe-inspired crowd. If our dream is singing, we see in our mind's eye a throng on their feet cheering as we belt out a powerful melody. Some of us dream simply while others of us dream with Technicolor ambition. But we all dream. It is our dreams that define our lives. It is our dreams that define the way we spend our time.

A set-apart young woman dreams differently than the rest of her female contemporaries. Instead of dreaming dreams that bring her to center stage in society's spotlight, she begins to dream God's dreams for her life. And God's dreams cause her to seek her Prince above all else, prior to all else, and at the risk of all else. She becomes fantastically preoccupied with her gallant Jesus.

To be a great ballet dancer demands time, and a lot of it. To develop an angelic singing voice takes countless hours of intensive training. To be great at anything demands great amounts of time. To be great at knowing our Prince is no different. It takes time—and lots of it. It demands that every last drop of our physical energy be focused on Him. He can't be conveniently fit into our lives; He must become what our lifestyles are built around. From the moment we wake up until the moment we go to sleep, He must become the center. And when He does, we quickly realize that God's dreams unlock the beauty of life itself.

6

Lily Whiteness
and Romance

Future Husband Application

It is a safe thing to trust Him to fulfill the desire which He creates.
AMY CARMICHAEL

$\mathcal{S}$O FAR I HAVE emphasized the importance of a love story with our true Prince being the centerpiece of our lives, hearts, actions, thoughts, and emotions. No human love story could ever compare to what awaits us in our inner sanctuary of intimacy with Him. So before I continue with this section, I must say once again—*only when we fall in love with Jesus Christ and build our lives completely around Him* can we experience human love and romance in its purest and most beautiful form.

Yet the more time I spent with my heavenly Prince, the more I realized that my heartfelt yearning for human love and companionship was a desire that He Himself had given me. I knew my Lord would be faithful, that He had a plan for this area of my life. But during the waiting process, my desire for human love did not disappear; it seemed only to increase. Waves of longing for a beautiful love story would almost overpower my emotions at times. It was at those moments that I knew I had to make a choice. I could either allow that desire to control me, or I could allow that desire to chase me deeper into the arms of my Prince. There were times when it would have been too easy to take matters into my own hands—for instance, by conveniently showing up at places where I knew there were plenty of cute, available, Christian young men and engaging in a little "harmless" flirting to see where it might lead. But the stronger the temptation, the more I learned to draw even closer to my Prince. I learned to not battle these longings alone, but rather to pour out my deepest desires to Him. And when I did, I felt His tender whisper upon my heart, giving me promises about my future husband and teaching me how to prepare for true love.

SET APART FOR MY FUTURE HUSBAND

"Just as you have become set apart for Me," He softly instructed, *"you must also become set apart for your future husband."* My commitment to my future spouse had always been to simply save my physical purity for him (a commitment that I had not lived out very successfully). But just as I was learning to live a *lifestyle of lily whiteness* for my Prince, I soon realized that my commitment to my future husband needed to go far beyond the physical realm. One day I stumbled upon a verse in Proverbs 31, the chapter in the Bible that describes a wife of godly character. "She does [her husband] good and not evil," it said, "*all* the days of her life" (verse 12). The words tugged at my heart. I had always done the bare minimum for that mysterious person out there somewhere known as my future husband. But now,

with the patient guidance of my Lord, I determined to live a life that would truly honor this man—to do him good and not harm—even before he came into my life.

My inner being had become a sacred sanctuary for my Prince, and it was in this inner sanctuary that I learned to be truly set apart for my future husband. I no longer pursued temporary relationships that chipped away at my heart, mind, emotions, and physical purity. Even in friendships with guys, I became extremely careful. I determined that the next time I would give *any* part of myself away would not be until I knew he was the one God had chosen for me to spend the rest of my life with. Even then, it would only be with the gentle, step-by-step guidance of my Lord. It was not always an easy commitment to keep, especially when a few amazing, godly young men came into my life and became some of my very close friends. They were the first guys I'd ever met who actually resembled the kind of person I wanted to marry. I battled with the fear that if I didn't try to make something happen with one of them, I would never find guys like them again. But honoring my future husband meant keeping my heart, emotions, body, and even my thought life in check—living a lifestyle of lily whiteness for him in every possible way. I felt assured that if my Prince had one of these particular guys in mind for me, He could orchestrate the love story in His own perfect way. In the meantime, my only job was to trust Him. And He was perfectly faithful.

TRASH AND TRUE LOVE

"How will I ever be able to explain all my past mistakes to my future husband?" asked Robin, a baby-faced nineteen-year-old from Connecticut. "How will he ever be able to forgive me?" The remorse that glistened in her eyes reminded me of the countless young women I've met over the past few years who have tearfully voiced that very same pain-filled question. "I know I can choose to live a lifestyle of lily whiteness for him from now on," they acknowledge, "but what about everything I've already given away?"

Amber, a tall, athletic volleyball player from Utah, had a different concern: "What if my future husband has already slept with other girls?" she wondered aloud. "How can I forgive him? How can I trust him?"

I can vividly recall the evening—shortly before we were engaged—when I sat down with Eric and tearfully confessed all the times I had carelessly given away pieces of my heart, mind, and body, tainting the pure treasure that had been meant only for him. I didn't want anything at all to hinder our intimacy in marriage, and I knew that I needed to ask his forgiveness for the times I had dishonored him in my past. I wanted to have his complete and full trust. I remember trembling as I spoke to him that night, wondering in the back of my mind how he would ever be able to forgive me. But when I finally glanced up at him, what I saw flooded my soul with peace. His tender, loving eyes were shining with the same gentle and willing forgiveness I had found in the eyes of my Prince. I was fully and completely forgiven. He did not see me as a tainted treasure but as a sparkling clean princess—his precious gift from God.

Soon it was *my* turn to offer forgiveness. Eric told me regretfully of all the times he had dishonored me as his future wife, about the other girls who had claimed pieces of his purity. But with the tender help of my Prince, I was able to completely forgive him. Eric had learned to love me with the unwavering love of Christ. There had come a time in his life when he made the choice to live in total faithfulness to his future spouse in every way—body, heart, and mind. Though he did not know my name at the time, he began to pray for me every day. He began to consider my feelings as he interacted with the opposite sex. He even wrote me love letters before we ever met!

Because of this, I did not question Eric's vow to be totally faithful to me once we were together. It was not a commitment he made out of emotion. It was not a promise he made in his own strength. His devotion to me was a reflection of the steady, unconditional love of our Prince. With our Prince at the center of our lives and our love, I knew that past mistakes had no hold over us. That night, through the tender grace of our Lord, we forgave each other completely. Our past sins have never since affected the breathtaking beauty of our love story. (Note: If God leads you to confess past impurity to your future spouse, it is not usually necessary or wise to go into specific detail about past sexual sins. Simply acknowledging your unfaithfulness and asking your spouse's forgiveness will accomplish what is needed for an unhindered love story.)

As we are shaped into the lily-white likeness of our Prince, we learn how to love as He loves: *unconditionally.* We learn how to forgive as He forgives: *fully and completely.* If your future husband builds his life around Jesus Christ, he will be shaped into the heroic likeness of his Lord. Your Prince will give him eyes to see you, not marred by a tainted past, but as the lily-white princess you have become.

PRACTICAL STEPS FOR LOVING YOUR FUTURE HUSBAND

When Jesus Christ scripts each detail of a romance and teaches us how to love like He loves, an unhindered, beautiful love story is possible *no matter what mistakes* we have made. Here are some practical ways to prepare for a Christ-centered love story, starting today.

Set-Apartness. Prayerfully consider your commitment to your future spouse. Ask yourself the questions: *Am I truly set apart for him? Or am I just doing the bare minimum for him by putting up a few physical and/or emotional boundaries in my life?* A lifestyle of lily whiteness for your future husband involves every part of your being—your thoughts, your emotions, your dreams, your imaginations, your habits, and your actions. It is not a set of rules to put up with; it is the natural outflow of a life that is being shaped into the lily-white likeness of your Prince. Being set apart for your future husband means loving him and honoring him, even before you meet him, by the way you live your life on a day-to-day basis. It is a sacrificial love, and it is certainly not easy. It often means giving up the short-term satisfaction of being affirmed by the opposite sex. And in today's world, that can be a very hard thing to give up.

In spite of the current cultural emphasis on feminine independence and even superiority, most of us as young women seem to be on an obsessive search for male attention and affirmation. We are desperate to prove to ourselves that we are desirable to the opposite sex. We are trained from a young age to walk, dress, flirt, talk, and act in ways that will make us attractive to the opposite sex. We are programmed to believe that if we are not constantly surrounded by lustful male attention, we have very little worth as young women. And while the culture encourages us to flaunt and experience our sexuality, we are also programmed to simultaneously shut off our hearts and emotions.

Television shows, movies, and magazines today showcase beautiful young women who haphazardly hook up with guy after guy. They are portrayed as the sexiest, strongest women of our times—able to "conquer" a guy sexually and yet keep their hearts completely unaffected by the whole experience. In reality, it doesn't work that way. Giving the most intimate part of ourselves to someone *always* opens up the heart and leaves us incredibly vulnerable, no matter how hard we try to stifle those "female" emotions. We were created to give ourselves fully and completely to only one person for a lifetime within the protective confines of a loving, trusting, committed, Christ-centered marriage. The millions of girls who try to live the sexually driven yet supposedly carefree life of a *Friends* character end up mutilating their hearts, bodies, minds, and futures.

But the pressure is everywhere—often even from parents and Christian leaders—to prove that we are active in our pursuit of the opposite sex. "Do you have a boyfriend?" was the never-ending question I heard from relatives, pastors, youth leaders, and friends throughout the early, young-adult years of my life. This, combined with the loud and incessant messages from the world around me, made me feel that I was incomplete as a young woman without touting a string of guys over my shoulder. I struggled with the inexplicable need to prove to everyone, including myself, that I was attractive to guys and that I could get a boyfriend anytime I felt like it. Thus, the habits formed. Flirting. Flaunting. Flings. Fantasies. When I made a commitment to live a set-apart life for my future husband, *all* of those habits had to die. I had to let go of my need to be affirmed by the opposite sex and trust that when my Prince brought my future husband into my life, it would be my lifestyle of *lily whiteness*—not culture-formed sex appeal—that he would find beautiful and attractive in me.

To become set apart for a future husband, we must really examine the way we relate to the opposite sex. Some soul-searching questions must be posed:

- *Do I seek male affirmation through flirting, hugging, touching, etc.?* (And we can't let ourselves draw the line at just flirting or physical stuff—we must take a look at our whole demeanor. It's possible that those cute puppy-dog eyes we always make or that sweet little innocent giggle could be our preferred method of turning heads!)
- *Do I draw guys' attention by showing off my body?* (You know, bending down to pick something up at just the right

moment, or wearing that oh-so-cute top that also happens to leave little to the imagination.)

- *Do I casually offer my heart, mind, emotions, and body to guys by jumping into short-term flings?*
- *Do I allow my mind to fantasize about guys I am attracted to?*
- *Do I offer too much of myself to guys, even in friendships?*
- *Am I willing to sacrifice pleasure, attention, affirmation, and temporary fulfillment to live a lifestyle of lily whiteness for the man I will spend the rest of my life with?*
- *Am I willing to allow my faithful Lord to bring a love story into my life in His own perfect time and way?*
- *Am I willing to hand over the pen of my love story to Christ and trust Him completely?*

A great way to solidify your decision to become fully set apart for your future spouse is to write him a letter. It doesn't have to be a long letter—just a few carefully chosen words that express your commitment to live a lifestyle of lily whiteness for him and your reasons for wanting to honor him completely with the way you live. It is a great idea to outline specific choices you have made, or have determined to make, in your life in order to honor him. Whenever you struggle with loneliness or begin to question your decision, pull out the letter and read it again. It can be used as a reminder of the sacrificial, unconditional love your Prince has for you. It can help you continually renew your decision to love your future spouse with the very same love.

🦌 TAKING OUT THE TRASH. More than likely, you have done things in your past that have dishonored your future husband, things that have tainted the treasure that was meant only for him by compromising the purity of your heart, mind, and/or body. If you have been following the suggestions of this book so far, then you've probably already taken those sins before your Prince, received His forgiveness, allowed Him to wash you clean, and removed them from your heart and life. If not, my first suggestion is to work through the material mentioned earlier in this book, entitled "Inner Sanctuary," which can be found under "Downloads" on the *Authentic Beauty* Web site at www.authenticgirl.com.

Healing in this area of our life begins with allowing our Prince to wash us clean, whiter than snow, and to remove sin's residue from our inner being. The same is true for things that have been done *to* us, such as rape, abuse, violence, even hallway teasing. The trauma of these experiences can stake a claim over our hearts, distorting our views about our purity and our potential for a beautiful love story. Only the healing, cleansing touch of our Prince can restore this part of who we are. And if we are willing to let Him do His work, we will be amazed at the freedom we discover.

But the question remains—what about your future husband? How do you ask *his* forgiveness for what you have done? How do you explain to him about abuse you suffered in your past? If he is not in your life yet, a practical solution is to write him a letter. If you have made mistakes in this area of your life, ask him to forgive you for dishonoring him. If you have suffered rape or abuse, express what happened and write about the cleansing, healing work of your Prince in this area of your life. (Your future husband will have to forgive those who wronged you, just as you have had to forgive them.)

When your future husband comes into your life, allow Christ to show you when the time is right to either give him your letter or sit down and talk with him in person about your past. A love story centered on Jesus Christ is guided and directed by Him every step of the way, and He is always faithful to gently show us what to say and when to say it. On the night I talked to Eric about my past, I was acutely aware of the surrounding, healing, loving presence of my Prince every moment of the conversation. Though it was painful, it was a conversation that only brought Eric and me closer to each other and to our Prince.

Your future husband—if he is fully surrendered and devoted to Jesus Christ—will be given eyes to see you for who your Prince has made you to be. With the help of the Lord, he will be able to forgive you completely, no matter what you have done. He will be able to forgive those who wronged you, no matter what has been done to you. Through the eyes of Jesus Christ, he will not see you as tainted or marred but as a beautiful, Christlike, lily-white princess.

It is also quite possible that your future husband has not kept himself completely pure for you. Most of us dream of marrying a man who has never given his heart, mind, or body to another woman. This is a natural, God-given desire. This is something worth praying and hoping for, and many times I have seen God answer that prayer. It is a standard worth motivating the men in your life to attain. And yet, if your God-written love story, like mine, takes place with someone who has not always honored you in the area of physical, mental, and/or emotional purity, He will grant you the grace to forgive. You must ask your Prince to teach you to love as He loves, to forgive as He forgave us, and to have eyes to see your future husband not for his failures and mistakes but for the heroic knight Jesus Christ is shaping him into.

CHAPTER SIX IN A NUTSHELL

Our girlish passion for Mr. Right can become either our poison or our prize. This craving for human companionship we all feel as young women can prove to be either our undoing or the key that unlocks all the beauty and dazzle of life. We long for a chivalrous prince. We make one of the defining decisions of our lives when we choose *where* to look for him. If we choose to look among the noble men of this earth, our girlish passion quickly becomes our poison. But if we look to fulfill that craving by giving our lives to our gallant heavenly Lover, we find both the key to unlock an eternal love life with Christ and the key to unlock amazing earthly love with a noble husband-to-be.

The extraordinary thing about earthly love is that it was invented by God. But He alone holds the keys to unlock its purpose and potential in our lives. God trains us as set-apart young women to be set apart not only for His enjoyment but also for the future enjoyment of an earthly husband. Just as He requires us to remove all other lovers from our lives to experience a love relationship with Him, He instructs us to do the same for our earthly lover. If we learn to be one-man women with our physical bodies, with our minds, and with our affections, we set the stage for an earthly love story that is out of this world. And if we never experience an earthly fairy tale, we have the privilege of being set apart for the greatest Husband who ever lived and experiencing the most fulfilling love story of all time. Intimacy with Him is worth every sacrifice we could ever make.

A Vision of Warrior Poets

by Eric Ludy

As a young woman, you probably spend a fair amount of time wondering what makes us guys tick. The answers to perplexing questions like why we guys get excited about things like burping contests, or why we feel extratough when we are drenched with sweat, may never be fully understood in this life. Despite this fact, I am a man who believes that young women *can* become better equipped to respond to young men in today's culture.

Leslie has requested that I add these "Studying Manhood" sections to this book, not only to help accent your understanding of young manhood, but also to help accent your understanding of young womanhood. As Leslie says, "A key ingredient to a girl becoming a woman is learning to truly understand the manhood of Christ and then learning to help the males in her life transform into Christlike princes."

If you take seriously these three lessons on manhood, you will know more about manhood than most guys alive today (that is truly sad, I know!). If you make the study of masculinity a serious endeavor, you can literally help to change the course of nations. We, as men, will rise to the expectations of the young women in our lives.

My hope is that what I share will help you better understand guys today—how we think, what we desire, and why we act the way we do.

More importantly, Leslie and I hope that these chapters will inspire you as a young woman to motivate the men in your life to become far better men—men like Jesus Christ.

MY INTRODUCTION TO TRUE MANHOOD

It was a number of years ago now that I first charged the fields of Bannockburn (on my noble steed, of course) alongside Sir Robert the Bruce. My Smurf-blue Scottish war paint made me look strangely akin to something out of Fraggle Rock, and I wore my plaid, Scottish, dresslike thingy proudly as I raised my fist and cried, "Freedom!" Brandishing my sword (as only true warriors can brandish), I challenged King Edward to fight: "You want a piece of me, Eddie boy?" I was an inspired man.

Yes, this was all in my imagination, but as I read the book *The Scottish Chiefs*, I was ready for battle. My hero, William Wallace, had just died a horrible death at the hands of the English, and his example of courage and daring burned within my soul. I wanted to follow him, I wanted to fight for him, and I wanted to die alongside him. As Sir Robert the Bruce was calling out for all Scottish patriots to join him in following Sir William Wallace's example, I found myself standing up and saying, "Count me in!" Of course, since the battle took place almost seven hundred years earlier, it was difficult for me to actually participate. It was in my imagination or nothing!

My generation of men rarely sees the blend of courage and kindness, of strength and sensitivity, of bravery and servanthood that we see in the fiery eyes of Sir William Wallace. It was while riding beside him into battle somewhere in the Scottish Highlands that I first grasped the marvel of a Warrior Poet. His countenance was calm but riddled with intensity. His sword was drawn, his cheeks suffused with blood, his lips silently moved to the mutterings of a prayer. He was the epitome of fearlessness in the face of the gravest danger. Yet, at the same time, he was the embodiment of heartfelt compassion.

Sir William showcased a manhood that honored and reverenced femininity and would give its life to protect the essence of it—a manhood that considered courage in the face of pain as one of the highest virtues, a manhood that valued spiritual pursuit, a manhood that esteemed purity of conscience and protection of the poor and weak. As I read about him, I asked myself over and over: *Who is this man? How can I get what he has?*

To this day, that picture of majestic man-ness, as portrayed in the life of William Wallace, leaves me awe inspired. On the wall next to my computer monitor I have pinned a scrap of paper to remind me daily of the kind of man I want to become. Though this scrap contains but a few hastily scrawled sentences, my melodramatic imagination goes back in time to witness the moment these captivating sentences were written. (They were actually written just a few years ago to include in the CD insert for the *Braveheart* soundtrack, but how boring is that?) I picture them being the last gasp of a bloodied Scottish noble. Fresh from the field of battle and sensing his life slipping from him, he scrawls these words (Scottish bagpipes play their soul-stirring tones in the background):

> In the year of our Lord 1314, patriots of Scotland, starving and outnumbered, charged the fields of Bannockburn. They fought like warrior poets. They fought like Scotsmen and won their freedom. Forever.[14]

Something deep inside me is touched by the feistiness of these words, by the raw strength and self-sacrifice portrayed in these few sentences.

So a dusty old book written in 1820 offered me more than just great literature. It gave me a version of manhood that I desperately desire to see formed within my life. Since first "meeting" Sir William Wallace, I no longer am interested in being just a male with muscles and a mustache (actually, I can't even grow a good mustache and, as my mom says, I am built more like a golfer than a football player). I now want to be a man of substance. I don't want to be just a boy who plays at manhood, but a Warrior Poet who lives it. And what I want you, as a young woman, to know is that a lot of young men are like me in needing a picture of what we *could* become. We desire to be so much more than we are today—we just don't know that we desire it. But it's the vision of what we could become that stirs the desire for the Warrior Poet to be formed within us.

HOW WARRIOR POETS ARE MADE

It seems to me that nearly every young woman with a pulse today has wondered if Warrior Poets still exist. Are Sir William Wallaces to be expected once every seven hundred years like one of those quixotic solar eclipses, or is it possible that the recipe for "majestic man-ness" could be cooked into *every* young man's heart and life?

Unfortunately, most of the young women I talk to believe in the one-extraordinary-man-every-seven-hundred-years theory. In fact, I've come to understand that girls today believe in Warrior Poets as much as they believe Santa Claus can touch his tongue to his belly button. Here's just a sampling of what I'm hearing girls say about the modern version of guyhood:

"Simply put," says Kirsti, a vivacious young girl with a knack for swing dancing, "guys are jerks!" (She adds, "I don't mean you, Eric!" after she makes her pronouncement, but the sting had already reached my heart.)

"I don't know," quips another college coed with bright red lips. "Don't guys, like, think about sex once every five seconds?" She furrows her eyebrows, crinkles her nose, and then adds her finishing thoughts as if she has just accepted defeat at the hands of Edward Longshanks. "I guess guys will always be guys. That's disgusting, but that's the way they are!"

I think I know why so many young women have these views of men: young men in my generation have been shaped by a warped pattern of manhood. It's no wonder that men today are so often referred to as jerks—the foundation of their manly behavior is self-serving and self-gratifying.

Being a man, I'm well acquainted with the perversion process. You see, we as young men desire to be "normal." Whatever our culture defines as normal behavior can very quickly become our manly pursuit. I was told somewhere in my junior-high years that having sex on the brain was a normal boyhood-to-manhood issue. I was told, even by women, that I, as a man, had only one thing on my mind. (Of course, that one thing was defined as sex, or possibly a better way of describing it: a fixation with the female body.) Well, if we as young men are interested in being normal, just hazard a guess as to what we are going to think about.

A dominant force behind the quality of modern masculinity in our culture is the expectations of modern women. The feminist movement led to great freedom for women, but not without cost. The great tragedy of feminism is that it has locked masculinity in a perverted cellar where it is nearly impossible for masculinity to transform itself.

It would be misleading to say to you that men don't have a weakness in the sexual-preoccupation department. But this weakness has been turned into an expectation. A young child may have a natural inclination to steal cookies from the cookie jar, but a good parent doesn't say, "Kids will be kids," and not correct the child and expect something better in the future. Men need someone to believe in them. They need someone to tell them that they *can* rise above this mediocrity. They need someone to tell them that they *can* have a lot more than "one thing" on their minds. They need someone to raise the expectations of their manhood. Believe it or not, we as men need *you*, a young woman, to help us find our way out of this spiritual gutter of cultural normalcy.

Leslie inspires me in my pursuit of manhood more than any other force, save the Spirit of God within me. I don't think I would be stretching it to say that Leslie's vision of manhood for me is as important as my vision of manhood for myself. I often like to say, "The words of my princess make me a prince."

It is *because* Leslie has a vision for me to be more than a burping and scratching male with only one thing on my mind that she enables me to become so much more. She has a vision to see me become a world changer, a man among men, a picture of her heavenly Bridegroom, her Prince and Lover—Jesus Christ. She believes in what manhood can be, she honors the way I'm uniquely crafted, she understands masculinity through God's perspective, and she expects me to pursue nothing short of total and complete man-ness. It's weird, but she gets just as excited about my "manly" quotes hanging around my computer monitor as I do. While for me they represent what I desire for myself, for her they represent what *she* desires for me. As a woman, she wants a Warrior Poet and nothing less. She wants a man willing to pour out his life for Jesus Christ, but she also wants a man who can enunciate his heart and show sensitivity to her world. Her gaze upon my masculinity is like lightning to my soul. Her expectations are my inspirations.

William Wallace in the book *The Scottish Chiefs* was actually a portrayal of Jesus Christ. The author purposely clothed the character of the stout-hearted Wallace with the world-altering manhood of Jesus Christ. It was that fresh picture of the manhood of Christ that radically altered my vision of what my personal masculinity could be shaped into. The author had a vision to raise the expectations of what men should declare as their minimum standard and what women should expect out of their men. The amazing thing about this author who wrote the book that shaped my vision of manhood and inspired the ultimate guy flick, *Braveheart,* is that he…well, *was a SHE*! Her name was Jane Porter. It was a *woman* with a correct vision of manhood that lit the flame of willingness within my heart to become all that God desired for me to be. I guess I could say that the words of a princess named Jane are helping to shape me into a prince like Jesus!

Putting It into Action

Here are four great ways to help shape young men into Warrior Poets:

1. *Practice making princes out of the men in your life.* Start with your dad and brother(s). If you can learn how to be a prince maker in your relationships with them, you will be off-the-charts amazing in your potential future relationship with your groom. Go out of your way to mention that you notice the things that they have done well (for example, mowed the lawn, barbecued some burgers, painted the kitchen, or swished a free throw) or the times you see them modeling a picture of manhood that you respect (being helpful, being courageous, being sensitive, or being humble.) Over time, as you gain even more of a vision for what a young man can become, you'll develop your own ways to draw majestic man-ness out of the guys in your life. It's the

words of our princesses that make us princes. We need to hear from you.

2. *Challenge men to a higher standard.* Just by guarding your heart and waiting for a Christlike Warrior Poet, you can challenge men to a higher standard without needing to say a word. When a guy realizes that you are holding out for a Christlike gentleman, it may be the motivation he needs to evaluate his own version of masculinity. There is no need to be aloof or distant toward less-than-Christlike guys. If you simply have a sweet, cheerful confidence in the standard you are holding out for, it can cause a guy to stop and think twice about his behavior. Maybe certain guys in your life showcase more of our culture's perversion than the inspirational manhood of Jesus Christ. If that's the case, when opportunity arises, verbally proclaim a higher level of expectation. Being critical or preachy won't be effective. Rather, in a lighthearted and friendly way, gently prod them toward something better. Here are a few samples of what it could look like, though you'll most likely have to adapt the language to fit your own way of communicating.

   a. *If they burp or do anything else in the gross family,* say very sweetly something like, "I've heard that burping is considered very attractive to the bearded, one-eyed, yak-worshiping women of Hanalei, but unfortunately most other girls don't find it very charming!"

   b. *If they hesitate to help someone in need,* comment (again very sweetly) something akin to, "This job demands a man with great strength and massive biceps," then look his way and, with a tilt of your head and adding a sighing lilt to your voice, say, "Ahhh, here is the man of bulging biceps who will surely save the day!"

c. *If they refer to womanhood in a derogatory fashion,* be quick to gently add, "I've heard that the men who speak highly of femininity are the ones who end up with the most beautiful wives."

d. *If they attempt to pressure you to sacrifice your sacred innocence,* quickly leave them in the dust, and in your parting say something like, "You have the potential to be a great man. And when you are, you will be a protector rather than a conqueror of a woman's innocence."

3. *Ponder the manhood of Christ.* Read both the book of Song of Solomon and the book of Revelation in the Bible. Reading those two books together, with the sole intention of seeing a picture of what Christlike manhood looks like, has an amazing impact. Song of Solomon gives a picture of Christ as a poet, a gentle encourager, and a servant-lover. Revelation provides a picture of Christ as a conqueror, a hero, a Warrior of warriors, and a King of kings. As a young woman, acquaint yourself with the ultimate Warrior Poet, Jesus Christ, and then you will know better what manhood is supposed to look like.

4. *Become a student of manhood.* If you make the study of manhood a lifetime research project, you will, in the process, become an amazing young woman. Start up a journal for yourself, titled something original like "My Study of Manhood." In it, write all your thoughts, observations, and discoveries about Christlike manhood. Ask God to begin to teach you how to appreciate manhood and see it the way He does. A woman who appreciates manhood is an instrument God will use to shape manhood. In fact, I keep a journal about womanhood. I know that sounds strange, but it's true. I began doing it a few years ago so I could better serve

Leslie and draw her out as a woman. In the process I have gained incredible insight into God's heart for womanhood, which makes me want to cheer *you*, a young woman, on to discover all that God has for you. This is one of the most practical things you can do to prepare yourself for marriage.

Jane Porter gave me the vision of Christlike manhood, and here I am, 150 years after her death, thanking her for her incalculable contribution to my life. Maybe you should consider making it one of your goals, as a young woman, that 150 years from now extraordinary Christlike man-ness will be a far more common thing thanks to the self-sacrifice of your life. As men, we would be eternally grateful.

romantic *mystique*

the mystery

of a set-apart

young woman

My beloved is mine and I am his;
he delights in the lilies.

SONG OF SONGS 2:16, NEB

7

Feminine Mystique

Discovering the Lost Art of Mystery

*The world-altering and life-giving secret that was kept hidden
through the ages, but is now made known to Christ's set-apart
ones, is simply this: Jesus Christ, your heavenly Prince, will
actually make your earthly body His royal residence! Yes, it's true!
The Prince coming to live within your sanctuary—this is the
world-altering secret that ushers in His kingdom.*

COLOSSIANS 1:26–27, PARAPHRASE[15]

*H*AVE YOU EVER longed to live
in a different era? I used to sigh wistfully every time I watched an old-
fashioned Jane Austen love story unfold on a movie screen. I would
gaze at the beautiful women in gorgeous, flowing gowns waltzing
around ballrooms with handsome, chivalrous men. I would float
away to that distant time, imagining I was there. Across the dance
floor, standing near the punch table, would be the man I secretly
loved. He was the perfect picture of a true gentleman. He would steal

a discreet glance at me and then quickly turn away, as if he felt it would not be appropriate to stare. I would pretend not to notice him, but my cheeks would flush with silent anticipation as I dared to hope that this gallant man might be interested in me.

When the party was over and I was preparing to leave, he would rush across the room to help me put on my wrap. Then he would offer me his arm and walk me to my carriage, gently helping me up the steps and onto the cushiony seat. Just before the driver pulled away, he would politely ask if he might call on me sometime. I would shyly smile, hesitate, and then softly answer, "Yes, I would like that." And as the horse clip-clopped through the cobblestone streets, my heart would soar with the thrill of a budding romance. The next day, at teatime, our maid would come to my room (where I would be sitting at my desk composing beautiful poetry with a quill pen) and announce that I had a gentleman caller waiting for me in the parlor. My heart would begin to beat with excitement, but as I slowly descended the staircase, my demeanor would be calm and dignified. The gallant man and I would sit across the room from each other, sipping slowly out of dainty teacups, shyly glancing at each other and talking about the weather. When I rose to summon the maid to replenish the plate of scones, he would, in an almost reflexive reaction of chivalry, stand until I had left the room.

Over the next few weeks and months, our love story would slowly blossom. Unlike a modern romance, we would not end up in the back row of a movie theater, passionately making out. We would not spend hours on the phone, sharing the deepest dreams, hopes, and desires of our hearts. We would not tenderly embrace every time we saw each other, whispering emotional sentiments in each other's ears. In fact, our love story would not be at all like today's hold-nothing-back version. It would be slow and delicate, like the gentle opening of a flower. Our romance would be surrounded by wonder and mystery. We would spend time together but would remain very cautious about speaking of our growing affections for the other. I would be careful not to allow him to see much of my inner emotions. I would not allow him to have my heart—or even see inside my heart—until I was absolutely certain he was worthy of such a sacred gift.

In the meantime, he would be gallantly working to win my heart. He would be sensitive, attentive, and patient, not making his love for me overtly obvious until he was sure I was ready. He would come to visit, but not every day, keeping me guessing—and hoping. He would send flowers occasionally and sometimes a beautifully scripted note that asked if I might grant him the honor of accompanying him to an upcoming ball. All the while, he would be the perfect gentleman, never asking or expecting me to give him what was not yet his to claim. He would treat me like a valuable, delicate treasure—and he would know that this treasure had not yet been given to him to hold.

Then one day we would be strolling along a garden lane in the early part of spring, and he would gently lead me to a bench beside a trickling brook. When I daintily sat down, my long dress flowing all around me, he would kneel, softly take my hand, and declare his ardent admiration for me. "You are a picture of true grace, dignity, and beauty," he would whisper eloquently. "You have fascinated me for months. The times we have spent together have only ignited my desire to spend my life discovering more and more about you." He would declare himself unworthy of the sacred treasure of my heart, but then say that he would be betraying his own heart if he did not ask me to be his wife. I would tearfully smile, whisper, "Yes," and then fully offer him the priceless gift of my tender heart—now and forever. And even after we were married (in a quaint cobblestone chapel wreathed with exquisite flowers), my gallant gentleman would still treat me with utter tenderness and respect—opening doors for me, standing when I left the room, and cherishing every moment with me as he continued to discover more and more about the mysteries of my heart.

Okay, I know that by now I might have you gagging, rolling your eyes, sarcastically groaning, "Dream on!" or wishing you could pat me on the head and inform me sweetly that I am completely deluded. Everything around us in today's world mocks such tales as prudish and old fashioned. We have seen too many burping and scratching versions of the males of the species to believe that gallant gentlemen truly exist anymore. Perhaps it is easier to say such dreams are childish. But although I know many young women who outwardly scorn all such Jane Austen romances, many of those same girls have secretly confided to me that deep down, they long for those days of gallant chivalry. Even though today it is not politically correct to admit it, there is something about those old-fashioned tales of "winning a heart" that spark a wistful desire within so many of us. I believe it is because such stories contain a vital element of true love that has, in modern-day culture, all but vanished from existence. This all-but-extinct aspect of love is something I like to call *romantic mystique*.

THE LOST ART OF MYSTIQUE

What is romantic mystique? Mystique means guarding what is sacred, protecting the essence of who we are from the inside out—our hearts, emotions, intimate thoughts, and physical bodies. A woman with mystique preserves the treasure of who she is, keeping herself set apart for one who proves he is worthy of such a gift. Feminine mystique is a lost art. Today it is far more vogue to hold *nothing* sacred than it is to protect our hearts, emotions, or bodies. It is even considered prudish or snobby to hold purity sacred and fool yourself into believing that there is actually a man out there somewhere who will value your heart as a treasure.

For many years, I bought into the lie that feminine mystique was an outdated, ridiculous concept. My thinking was shaped by the culture around me. Girls who had no sense of mystery about them—the ones who aggressively pursued guys and willingly gave everything they had to one guy after another—were the girls who seemed to get all the male attention. The culture told me time and time again that feminine mystery only made a girl look undesirable to the opposite sex. Like many other warped perceptions in my life, this mentality was imparted to me at a young age. I remember a conversation that took place among some of my female peers when I was just fifteen years old.

"I lost my virginity last night," Tanya announced indifferently, as she opened a packet of mustard and squirted it on her six-inch turkey sub. A group of us were sitting on the warm grass outside the huge double doors leading to the gym, taking our lunch break. We were eating lazily, trying to soak up as much sun as we could before we were forced to return to our dungeonlike classrooms for the rest of the day. Our conversation had been dull for the most part since it was the week of midterms and our brains felt like mushy piles of cream of wheat. Tanya's statement, however, steered things into the realm of the interesting, and all eyes turned to her as she ripped open a minibag of Cool Ranch Doritos.

"Congratulations," Ashley told her in a dry voice. "It's about time, that's all I can say."

"Like you can talk, Little Miss 'I've Had Sex Two Whole Times,'" Tanya replied sarcastically. Then with a triumphant gleam in her eye she added, "Besides, I bet *you* never did it with three of his *friends* in the room!"

Suddenly, if our little group wasn't already awake, we woke up. The girls erupted into incredulous laughter and shouts of "*What? Are you kidding?!*" Tanya just smirked at our outburst.

"Come on, Tanya! Tell us what happened!" begged Vanessa, putting down her Diet Mountain Dew and leaning in.

Tanya smiled slyly and explained how she had told her boyfriend, Jordan, that she wanted to have sex with him—and that she didn't care if his friends were there when it happened. (Somehow this twisted scenario had involved a bet between Tanya and her older sister, Tracy.) Jordan's parents were out of town, so Tanya, Jordan, and three of his buddies got drunk, blasted Aerosmith, congregated in the bedroom, and let depravity take its course.

"I can't believe you!" Ashley laughed incredulously, shaking her head. "I would totally *freak* if Seth's friends stood there and watched us! Didn't that, like, bother you at all?"

Tanya just shrugged. "Not really," she answered flippantly, "I mean, I'm totally comfortable with my body—why should I care who sees me have sex? It's not like it's a big deal or something."

"Wow, I totally admire you," said Vanessa wistfully. "I wish I could be that relaxed about...you know, *stuff.* I don't think I could do something like that."

Tanya shrugged again. "You just have to stop being so uptight," she said patronizingly.

"That is so good, Tanya, that you're so comfortable with your body like that—I mean, you are really mature!" Ashley said approvingly. She took a bite of her meatball sub, chewed for a minute, and then asked, "So what did Jordan think after it happened? Is he totally in love with you now or what?"

Tanya paused and took a long swig of her Sprite. She seemed to be trying to suppress some new emotion. Her eyes became clouded, and she swallowed hard. Finally, she looked back at us with a confident smile. "We broke up this morning," she said carelessly. "He likes someone else."

The group was silent for a minute, digesting this unexpected piece of information, unsure what to say. Finally, Vanessa sympathetically murmured, "Wow. I'm so sorry."

But Tanya looked annoyed. "I don't give a rip," she retaliated defiantly. "It's not like I'm one of those crybabies who's like, 'Oh, Jordan, I gave you my virginity—now you have to love me forever!'" She rolled her eyes at the very thought of such a ridiculous sentiment.

Ashley nodded in agreement. "Yeah, that is so smart. Sex shouldn't be some gushy emotional thing; it's just about enjoying the moment, you know? You should have the freedom to hook up with different guys whenever *you* decide to—don't let any of them have control over you…"

At that point, I dragged myself to my feet and announced that I had to go change for volleyball. As I walked away, the little group was still passionately exhorting one another about the freeing and admirable art of sexual detachment. Girls like Tanya were lifted up as examples to the rest of us. They had matured to the point where they had become comfortable with their bodies; they had supposedly taken full control of their own lives and emotions. The goal seemed to be to have *as little* feminine mystique as possible and to toss away those ridiculous, fairy-tale notions of chivalry and true love.

Fortunately, I had other influences in my life, like my parents and church leaders, who went out of their way to contradict the anti-sacred message I was hearing from society on a daily basis. "Your virginity is a sacred gift," I was told, "a treasure to protect and one day give to your future husband."

Something, however, was lacking in the modern-day Christian approach. The Christian community tended to focus on the need to protect *only* virginity. There was no concept of romantic mystique involved! Protecting one's virginity became a technical physical boundary with very little beauty or romance surrounding the whole idea. Maybe it was just my own spiritual immaturity at that time, but somehow, between my youth pastor's purity pep talks, Christian dating books, and Christian young-adult magazines, I fell under the assumption that as long as I did not *technically* have sex, I was "doing the right thing" and guarding a sacred gift for my future husband. Apparently, that was the highest level of feminine mystique I could reach.

I was not the only one who adopted this assumption. Many of my Christian friends thought, like me, nothing of tossing around their hearts, emotions, and bodies in relationships with guys, wholeheartedly believing that they were protecting their sacred gift as long as they remained technical virgins.

Megan, a vivacious cheerleader from my youth group, frequently bragged about how she and her long-term boyfriend, Chris, "respected each other" enough to save sex for marriage. Chris often stayed over at Megan's house, and they would lie in bed together all night in each other's arms, usually with very little clothing on, but apparently they had enough self-control not to *technically* have sex.

"Our wedding night is going to be so special because we're waiting," Megan would declare happily. But sometimes I wondered if there would really be all that much difference between their wedding night and every other night they had fallen asleep in each other's arms. What exactly was going to be so special about their wedding night? Megan and Chris had a version of protecting the sacred that was a far cry from the days when even holding hands was a carefully guarded and deeply cherished expression of affection.

Sarah, a pretty redhead who also attended my youth group, fell in love with Kip, one of the hot young interns at our church. She spent a year drooling over him before he ever looked in her direction. When he finally showed some interest, she walked around in a stupefied, euphoric daze for weeks. "Kip called me last night," she would gush breathlessly. "We talked for five hours! He is so sweet! I feel like I can tell him *anything!*" And she did. Sarah opened her heart to Kip like a floodgate over the next two months, pouring out her dreams, desires, hopes, fears, longings, and intimate thoughts to him until there was almost nothing about her he did not know. Everything seemed perfect until Kip became interested in someone else and very politely told Sarah that the passionate midnight chats had to end. Sarah was crushed. "I can't figure out why I'm so upset," Sarah confided to me one day. "It's not like I had sex with him or anything—we never even kissed! But for some reason, I still feel like Kip took a part of me I can never get back." Sarah's utter devastation over losing this platonic relationship made me realize that there was a lot more to guarding your sacred treasure than simply not having sex with someone.

One by one, I saw my Christian friends mirror my own experience in relationships: carelessly giving themselves to guys physically or emotionally (even though many of us technically remained virgins) only to end up feeling used and heartbroken in the end. The typical Christian version of protecting the sacred made me think of a little girl clinging to a rose in the middle of a vicious hurricane—the wind sweeps away all the petals, and when the storm dies down, she is left holding only the shriveled bare stem, which has been stripped of all its beauty. Though I knew it was a significant step up from Tanya's careless, drunken, one-night-stand approach, the Christian worldview only protected the *sexual act* as sacred—and nothing else. No beauty, wonder, or mystery surrounded the modern-day Christian version of romance. The more I observed this approach, the more it seemed to offer nothing more than a second-rate, watered-down version of romance. It did not hold even a trace of a Jane Austen love story.

WHERE MYSTIQUE BEGINS

There is so much more to feminine mystique than technical physical purity. Feminine mystique begins with guarding the most precious part of our existence: our intimacy with our Prince. (And our Prince, by the way, is the most gallant, chivalrous Gentleman of all time!) As we spend time in His presence, we become more like Him. As we become more like Him, we learn to guard what is sacred—just as He does. As His cherished princesses, we learn to protect the essence of who we are rather than letting it be trampled in the mud. We learn to keep the most intimate aspects of our being set apart for the eyes of our Prince alone.

Eric and I have created a "sacred sanctuary" in which to nurture intimacy in our marriage. Our home has become a private retreat, hidden away from the outside world; it is a set-apart haven where we can truly rest and enjoy each other. We work hard to protect our sanctuary. We say no to many outside invitations and commitments just so we can keep most of our evenings free for spending time nurturing our relationship—reading, listening to music, talking, or just being together. Certain rooms in our house are guarded extra carefully, like our bedroom. We keep the phone, mail, newspaper, computer, laundry, undone projects, and anything work related *out* of that room at all times. We keep the atmosphere in that room clean, fresh, and romantic with candles, soft music, and flowers. We don't invite friends or family into that room. We don't have business discussions in that room. We don't try to strategize or solve life's problems in that room. It is a sacred sanctuary—a set-apart place for nurturing our intimacy together. It must be carefully protected from outside intrusions and distractions. It must be kept hidden from the outside world.

What if our sacred sanctuary was not kept hidden from the outside world? Imagine a husband and wife trying to enjoy an evening of intimacy in a house with no walls. The moment they tenderly embrace, the delivery guy shows up with a large pepperoni pizza and informs them that they owe him $17.95. The little Domino's car drives away, and the couple tries to pick up where they left off. But just as they are gazing lovingly into each other's eyes, a carpet-cleaner salesman starts yelling excitedly at them, "How would you like to have four rooms cleaned for the price of three?" It takes about fifteen minutes to convince him that they are not interested in his services. As soon as they get rid of him, they once again attempt to get back in a romantic mood. But after a few minutes, their next-door neighbor appears, asking if she might borrow a cup of sugar. Once her measuring cup is full, she decides to stay and chat for a while, completely oblivious to the fact that the couple wants to be alone.

Needless to say, without protective walls around their sanctuary, intimacy between this husband and wife wouldn't be possible. For intimacy to flourish, both in a marriage and in a relationship with our Prince, our sacred sanctuary must be protected at all costs.

It is time for us to tune out the culture's insistent message that nothing we have is sacred. Whether or not a modern-day Jane Austen romance—with its chivalrous men and mysterious women—is really possible in today's world, there is one thing I *am* sure of: a far more breathtaking, beautiful, intimate love story with the ultimate, perfect Gentleman *can* be ours. Intimacy with Him is a precious, inestimable treasure—a treasure worth protecting with our very lives.

PROTECTING OUR SANCTUARY

Back in the days of gallant knights, enemies would storm the castle in an attempt to overthrow a kingdom. The castle was the center of the kingdom. It was the place where the king and his nobility dwelled, the place where the valuable treasures were kept, and the place where the kingdom's laws were made and plans executed. If the castle were overtaken, the kingdom would be destroyed. So it doesn't come as a surprise that extreme measures were taken to protect the castle at all costs. High, protective walls were built around the entire castle. A wide moat of water allowed people to enter and exit only by a drawbridge that was controlled by extremely cautious guards. Massive, solid-iron gates were positioned at the castle entrance and locked securely with heavy chains. The surly gatekeeper guarded the key with his very life. All through the day and night, legions of the kingdom's most skilled fighters were posted to prevent intruders from entering.

To guard our own sacred sanctuary, we must be just as aggressive as a king protecting his kingdom. If sturdy borders are not created around our sanctuary, sin can all too easily sneak back in and destroy the sacred intimacy we share with our Prince.

With the tender guidance of my Prince, I learned how to build protective walls around my sanctuary. My first step was developing "eagle eyes" toward sin, keeping watch like the castle guard, alert to any sign of the approaching enemy. Developing eagle eyes meant sharpening my ability to notice any hint of compromise in my life and dealing with sin instantly and completely.

By taking out the trash and removing the other lovers, I had dealt with the more obvious sins and past baggage that had controlled much of my heart. Now I needed to learn the skill of constant watchfulness to make sure the old thoughts and habits did not try to sneak back in. I also needed to learn to deal with the subtle compromises that had become a part of my everyday life.

I had spent much of my young adult life measuring my standards for integrity against everyone around me. When it came to guy-girl relationships, I figured that since I had kept my technical virginity, I was doing much better than a majority of my female peers who had slept with multiple guys by the time they were sixteen. When it came to music, I reasoned that I mostly listened to Christian bands and therefore was far better off than the majority of people my age who had no problem listening to raunchy, perverted lyrics. When it came to honesty—well, I only exaggerated a few meaningless details here and there; I never actually told "real lies." And the list went on. But soon my Prince showed me that my standards for integrity should be measured not against the world around me or even against Christian leaders, but only against His brilliant, flawless righteousness.

The more time I spent in the presence of my Prince, the more time I spent studying His Word, the more time I spent in stillness and prayer, the more I became aware, on a daily, hourly, and minute-by-minute basis, of the subtle compromises I often allowed to creep into my life. I began consciously running my thoughts, words, and actions through a series of internal questions: *Is what I am saying or doing right now completely honoring to my Prince? Is what I am looking at or listening to glorifying to Christ?* This was not a form of paranoia that interfered with my ability to live a peaceful, happy existence. It was merely a new *awareness* of the way I was living my life, motivated out of deep love for my Prince and a longing to protect the sacred inner sanctuary He had given me.

Here are a few examples of the subtle sins I had to learn to cleanse from my daily life:

Gossip. Though it had not been my habit to maliciously gossip about people, I hadn't seen any harm in engaging in a little light-hearted banter about someone's annoying social habits or irritating quirks. It was the kind of conversation that usually began with someone saying, "Not to be mean or anything, because I really like so-and-so, but have you ever noticed how she always does such and such?" Since this kind of discussion often took place among church friends, I had somehow felt it was justified. Yet I finally realized that this was something that did not reflect the likeness of my Prince, and soon I determined not to participate in or even listen to *any* form of gossip, no matter how innocent it seemed.

Selfishness. Surrounded by a culture that constantly gives the message, "Take care of yourself," I easily missed the fact that taking care of myself often translated into nothing but pure, old-fashioned self-ishness. Sure, I did a few "unselfish" things during my week, like tipping my waiter a little extra or letting fellow drivers into my lane when they were trying to merge with traffic. But those were fairly painless sacrifices to make. I soon began to realize just how self-focused I was when it meant having to give up personal comfort. If my parents were cleaning the garage or working in the yard and I was curled up on the couch with a book, all too often I conveniently pretended not to notice that they could use some help. If our small-group Bible study had planned to spend all Saturday sorting canned food in a homeless shelter's dirty warehouse, I would often find an excuse to miss out on the tedious, exhausting work, and if I did show up, I would be inwardly moaning and groaning about having to give up my weekend. Gradually, as my intimacy with my Prince deepened, I learned to recognize selfish attitudes. I worked on being willing to give up personal comforts in order to serve others so that, in the process, I could become more and more like Him.

Materialism. Like selfishness, materialism is so ingrained in modern-day American culture that it often goes unnoticed in our personal lives. I had grown up in a school system with kids from well-off families, and many of my high-school friends were given an endless supply of designer clothes, high-tech gadgets, and "toys"—including expensive new cars as soon as they got their driver's licenses. The fact that my parents did not spoil me in this way had always convinced me that I was not materialistic. But then I began to notice, as I walked through the mall on weekends or paged through beauty and fashion magazines, that a desire had been created within me to never be content with what I had—to always want more. I was not comfortable unless I had the latest shoes or jeans or sunglasses—and I usually found ways to get the things I wanted. I realized that materialism had become an unhealthy pursuit, a priority that I often built my life around, something that continually occupied my thoughts. I had to learn to make a conscious effort to take my focus off always getting more in the way of material things and instead focus on enjoying the amazing, *eternal,* priceless treasures my Prince had given me through the sacrifice of His very blood.

Laziness. Many of us frequently lament, "I really wish I could, but I just don't have *time* to spend alone with Christ every day!" Even though we might be busy, a closer look at our daily schedules might reveal that lack of discipline, *not* lack of opportunity, keeps us from spending time alone with our Prince. Being a hard-working, Type A personality, I would never have thought the word *laziness* could apply to me. But I finally realized that it was laziness that kept me from developing the discipline of going to bed at a reasonable hour so that I could get up early enough to have a long, focused period of time with my Prince. It was laziness that kept me from truly learning how to *study* my Bible rather than just skim over a few proverbs in the morning. It was even laziness that kept me from pursuing deeper relationships with my family members. I had to learn to aggressively shake off my lazy habits and actively discipline my life around my true priority: intimacy with my Prince. Like training for the first time to get into excellent physical shape, gaining true discipline was often painful and uncomfortable. But eventually, focused discipline began to replace lazy habits. Every area of my life, especially my relationship with my Prince, was incredibly strengthened as a result.

Self-Pity. Self-pity is one of the most dangerous attitudes to allow into our lives. It is one thing to become periodically sad when we are disappointed or hurt by something that happens to us. But continually wallowing in our own misfortune, allowing ourselves to moan and groan about every outward struggle we face, is extremely dangerous. It blinds us to see the needs of others, and worse, it keeps us focused on ourselves instead of on our Prince. Having made the difficult decision not to pursue temporary guy-girl relationships, I found it easy to lie awake in bed at night and feel incredibly sorry for myself that I currently did not have someone to share my life with. After I pulled away from many of my former shallow friendships, it was easy for me to become depressed about having to spend so much time alone. My Prince began to teach me how to recognize these emotional slumps as nothing more than ugly self-pity and to combat those internal pity parties by finding creative ways to bless or serve someone else. I was amazed at the joy I found in simply investing my time and energy in other people. It was usually just little things, like spending time getting to know one of my younger brothers in a deeper way or cooking a meal for a bedridden woman from church. My brothers and I began to visit a local hospital to sing for terminally ill respiratory patients a couple of times a month. I learned that when I invested myself in serving people (especially those who had far worse problems than I did!), my self-pity quickly faded into oblivion.

PRACTICAL STEPS FOR PROTECTING OUR SANCTUARY

Several years after beginning this process of protecting my sanctuary, I still have to guard against subtle compromises in my life. My weaknesses are still present, but I work to build my life around a constant *watchfulness,* always on the lookout for sins that try to creep in and clutter up my sacred sanctuary. I have found that setting aside times for soul searching is extremely helpful. Just a few moments of stillness with my Prince, asking Him to search my heart and gently point to any area of compromise that has been allowed to sneak in.

The subtle compromises that often sneak into *your* life might be very different from mine. But regardless of what our individual weaknesses might be, it is crucial to develop eagle eyes toward any and every sin that tries to encroach upon our inner sanctuary. It is important that we develop daily awareness of our motives, thoughts, attitudes, actions, and words—continually asking if what we are thinking, saying, and doing is a reflection of our Prince. When we notice an un-Christlike thought, action, or motive, it is vital that we deal with it immediately by repenting, asking Him to wash us clean, and actively adjusting our lives in whatever way is necessary to avoid that compromise from this day forward. As we learn to carefully, constantly protect the sacred treasure of unhindered intimacy with our heavenly Lover, the matchless beauty of feminine mystique will make its unmistakable mark upon our lives.

CHAPTER SEVEN IN A NUTSHELL

We humans get eerily protective of things sometimes. For instance, we will break an arm to preserve a dried-up wad of gum that once inhabited the smacking jowls of Brad Pitt. We'll spend hundreds of dollars on eBay to buy a signed baseball that was used in the World Series. We will go to extreme lengths to protect and preserve things that we perceive as having great value.

Believe it or not, this human tendency was given to us by God for an important purpose. But sin has warped and twisted it, teaching us to claw for worthless mementos while we trample underfoot everything that is truly sacred. When our Prince takes ownership of our lives, one of the first things He does is recalibrate our sense of value. I guess you could say He puts Brad's wad of gum into its proper place (the trash can!) and trains our eyes to recognize what is *really* of value. Then He trains us to go to extreme lengths to protect and preserve these supremely valuable things.

As set-apart young women, we must learn to guard one thing above all others: our sacred inner sanctuary. This holy chamber is the residence of our Prince; it is His imprint upon our souls. It is there that we meet Him; it is there that we share our love with Him. We must consider the value of maintaining this set-apart atmosphere for the Prince worthy of our very lives. For when our sanctuary is preserved, so is our love relationship with Christ. And there is absolutely nothing more valuable that that!

8

Battle Secrets

Winning the War Against Compromise

[Spiritual growth] is a question of obedience...
turn away for one second from obedience,
and instantly darkness and death are at work.

OSWALD CHAMBERS

WHEN I WAS SIXTEEN, I attended a purity banquet for teen girls at a local church. The guest speaker was a woman in her midforties with a confident expression on her dramatically made-up face. The program stated that she was going to tell the testimony of her love story—how and why she had remained pure for her husband until marriage. The other girls at my table were, like me, eager to hear an example of someone who had effectively resisted sexual temptation. In the world we lived in, such success stories were few and far between.

The woman held our attention as she told us about a wonderful

Christian guy she dated in college. "We were really attracted to each other," she said proudly (as if to clarify that most dating couples are only marginally attracted to each other). "We were alone together at my house one night when no one was home," she continued, "and while we were sitting together on the couch, things started to get really physical between us." She went on to say that just before the situation "really got out of control," she and her boyfriend suddenly heard the garage door open. Her older sister just happened to be coming home early from softball practice and arrived in the nick of time to stop them from "falling into sin." The couple quickly rebuttoned their clothes and frantically tried to restore their disheveled appearances just as her sister walked through the door. The speaker then paused and smiled affectionately at the memory. "God knew what we were about to do," she told us confidently, "and He provided a way out, just like He says in His Word. God always provides a way for us to flee from temptation!"

Despite the speaker's swelling pride over her "success story," the truth is that she and her boyfriend were not fleeing from temptation at all—they were willingly walking right into temptation and giving sin an open invitation to take over. Her story was not an example of successful purity; it was an example of successful distraction. Modern-day Christianity often leads us to believe that fleeing from temptation is nothing more than passively waiting for sin to find us and then expecting God to provide a way out at the last possible minute. But to flee from something means to immediately turn and run—not walk—as fast and as far as you can in the opposite direction. To effectively protect our inner sanctuary, we must not wait until sin has already begun to take over, but instead learn to immediately and aggressively respond to every hint of temptation with what I like to call the sudden-death technique.

THE SUDDEN-DEATH TECHNIQUE

Have you ever wondered why so many Christian leaders who outwardly live such pure and godly lives seem to suddenly fall into sin? There are plenty of heartbreaking examples of this in American churches today: the pastor who has an affair with a woman in his church; the youth leader who molests a boy from his youth group; the Christian singer who becomes obsessed with pornography. Despite how suddenly it seems to happen, the truth is that falling into sin does not come suddenly at all. Sin does not sneak up behind us and take hold of us unsuspectingly; it is allowed into our lives every time we choose not to flee from temptation.

The only effective way to deal with temptation toward sin is to give it no opportunity to take hold of our minds or hearts in the first place. Temptation, like a potted plant, cannot grow without our help. But the moment we allow it to take root within our hearts and feed it with our weak choices, it flourishes, eventually giving birth to ugly, controlling sin that overgrows our inner sanctuary. Only when we refuse to give temptation life will it suffocate. This is the sudden-death technique: never even giving temptation a chance to live inside us. Every temptation, however, comes with a crucial moment of decision—and that's when we choose whether to let it live or die.

CLARE, AN ENERGETIC young woman in her sophomore year of college, told me the sad tale of losing her virginity to a heartbreaker named Dale. Clare had come to Christ at an early age, had grown up in church, and was the worship leader for a Christian student group on her campus. Remaining pure for her husband was never a question in Clare's mind. She had always planned on saving her virginity for her wedding night and had even taught on purity for a teen girls' Bible study at her church. Out with her friends one Friday night, someone suggested going to a movie—a sweet-looking romantic comedy that had just hit theaters. As Clare watched the touching love story unfold on the screen, she found herself longing for that kind of intimacy and companionship in her own life. She had struggled with insecurity about her appearance and personality for many years and often wondered if she would ever find a guy who would love and appreciate her.

As the movie's heroine discovered true love, Clare felt a restlessness stir in her heart. Why couldn't she find that kind of relationship? She was tired of being alone. When a sex scene came on the screen, Clare noticed how tender and loving the experience seemed and began to wonder what the harm really was in expressing love for someone physically before marriage. It seemed so natural and beautiful. She left the theater that night smiling and chatting with her friends but inwardly weeping with desire for a man who would love her like that.

That night she lay in bed, trying to pray. Instead, she found her mind wandering, fantasizing about the guy from the movie, imagining that he was gazing into her eyes with passionate desire and tenderly running his finger softly down the side of her cheek. Her heart and body surged with desire. For that kind of man, Clare decided, she would do anything. A stab of guilt tugged at her heart as soon as that thought entered her mind. What about her commitment to keeping herself pure until marriage? She told herself she shouldn't be thinking this way, but the conviction was short-lived. One more mental image of the actor's smoldering gaze, and she quickly surrendered to another hour of mentally creating elaborate romantic fantasies with him before drifting off to sleep in a happy daze.

A few weeks later, Clare met Dale. When his piercing blue eyes met hers, her heart began to pound with longing. He was confident, attractive, and strong—the kind of man she had been fantasizing about every night for the past several weeks. When Dale asked her out, she felt her knees go weak with excitement. In the back of her mind, a tiny voice warned her to be cautious, but Clare paid no attention—she was too overwhelmed with the thought that her romantic dreams might actually be coming true.

After several weeks of dating Dale, Clare found herself in a spiritual dilemma. She was caught between her childhood commitment to purity and her intense desire for intimacy with Dale. He was charming—*too* charming. Clare felt like putty in his hands each time they were together. When she was near him, all logic and reason seemed to vanish; intense, uncontrollable emotions and desires seemed to take over her mind and body. At night as she drifted off to sleep, it was now Dale's face that she pictured as she invented her exotic, romantic fantasies. She knew that soon it wouldn't be only in her dreams that Dale would try to entice her to give herself to him in the heat of passion. In her heart she knew this would violate her commitment to purity, but every ounce of her being rebelled against the idea of saying no to Dale.

Clare tried to pray about her dilemma. She tried to seek advice from other girls in her Christian student group. But the more she prayed and talked and thought about Dale, the more it seemed to cause her imagination to awaken—vivid images of passion began to fill her mind on a continual basis. Then Dale invited Clare to spend the weekend with him at his uncle's vacant beach house. It took less than ten seconds for Clare to say yes.

"I never should have let myself go away with him that weekend," Clare lamented as she finished telling me her story. "I was so weak that the moment we were alone in the house, I just gave right in to temptation!"

When did Clare's first moment of decision really happen? At first glance it would seem to be the moment when she was alone in the beach house with Dale. Or maybe it was when he asked her to go away with him for the weekend, knowing where it would lead if she said yes. But looking closer at her story, I believe she had given in to temptation long before either of those crucial moments. When she saw that movie with her friends, there was the temptation to become discontent with her single life and her commitment to purity. She gave in. When she lay in bed that night, there was the temptation to allow her mind to fantasize about unbridled passion with a seductive man. She gave in. When she met Dale and looked into his piercing eyes, there was the temptation to throw caution to the wind and jump into a relationship with him, being led only by her emotions. She gave in. When she spent time with Dale, there was the temptation to ignore common sense and surrender to her surging physical and emotional desires. She gave in. When she prayed or talked or thought about Dale, there was the temptation to dwell on mental images of physical passion with him. She gave in. What had started as a tiny seed of temptation was allowed to take root in Clare's heart and mind. Each time she surrendered to it, it grew stronger and more controlling. Long before that final moment of decision at Dale's beach house, sin was already dominating her life.

In today's world, allurement toward sin is *everywhere*. We live in a culture that tries continually to pull us *away* from our Prince. Temptation often comes when you least expect it—while you are innocently chatting with friends, or relaxing in front of a movie, or even listening to the words of a respected teacher.

It starts with a subtle voice in the back of your mind, enticing you with dangerous little thoughts: *Look at her; she's doing it and she seems to be just fine! What is really so wrong with a little harmless flirting?* Or, *My life would be so much better if I could just be in a relationship with him. Maybe he's not the perfect Christian, but I'm sure I would be a good influence on his life if we were together.* Or, *If a leader I respect says it is okay, who am I to argue? The leader knows so much more than I do.* Or, *I've already messed up so many times—it's too late for me anyway, so why should I bother trying to live differently?*

It is at that *first moment of decision*—not several stages down the road—when we must apply sudden death to temptation before it ever has the chance to plant itself within our hearts and grow into sin. That first moment of decision is the time to flee—not to wait or hesitate, but to turn and run in the opposite direction. The moment we stop and listen to the voice of temptation, rather than immediately shutting it out of our hearts and minds, is the moment it plants its deadly seed within us and begins to gain control. In this life, temptation is inevitable. It is the *giving in* to temptation, even for a moment, that so quickly leads to deadly sin.

A devoted young college student, John Stam, who later gave his life for Christ on the mission field in China, once wrote about the two roads we must choose between whenever we are faced with any kind of temptation to sin. The first road John called "Seven Awful Steps Downward," and he describes each step on this road. The following is a paraphrase:

Step one: Adopting a careless attitude toward sin.

Step two: Giving in to sin.

Step three: Habitually giving in to sin.

Step four: Surrendering to sin.

Step five: Abandoning God for a life of sin.

Step six: Becoming a tool of Satan to tempt others to sin.

Step seven: Hell. And you do not have to die in order to get there. Hell is character as well as location. The person who hates everything that God loves is in hell now, and hell is in him or her.

The second road John called "Seven Glorious Steps Upward," and again he describes each step. The following is a paraphrase:

Step one: Developing a resistant attitude toward sin—determining that sin will not gain control over you.

Step two: Overcoming sin by faith in Christ. Successfully fleeing from temptation—saying no to the desire or opportunity to sin.

Step three: A lifestyle of victory over sin. Habitually saying no to the desire or opportunity to sin. The strength that comes from one victory helps in overcoming the next temptation.

Step four: Discovering the "abiding life," the "victorious life," the "exchanged life." It has been termed many things by many different Christians through the ages, but in short, it is a life of intimate acquaintance with the grace of Christ and the empowerment that comes when His Spirit gains full access to your life.

Step five: Entrance into even deeper fellowship with Christ. It started with your trusting God—now God entrusts His kingdom treasures to you. You are set apart for His enjoyment and for His service.

Step six: Becoming one whom God calls on to do great and mighty things for His kingdom. A set-apart existence that values Christ over life itself and is willing even to suffer and die to carry out the King's bidding.

Step seven: Heaven. And you do not have to die in order to get there. Heaven is character as well as location. The person who devotedly loves everything that God loves is in heaven now, and heaven is in him or her.[16]

For much of my life I thought that struggling with the same sins over and over was just a normal part of the Christian experience. When my Prince began to teach me how to protect my inner sanctuary, I realized that, when it came to temptation, there were only two roads for me to choose from: "Seven Steps Downward" or "Seven Steps Upward." And I could not be on both roads at the same time. Instead of just hoping that I didn't end up on the wrong road, I began to retrain my heart and mind to recognize the very first step downward—having a careless attitude toward sin. This was difficult at first, because the Christian culture I was surrounded by all too often portrayed a careless attitude toward sin, like that memorable speaker at my teen girls' purity banquet. Instead of realizing that she and her boyfriend never should have gotten into that situation in the first place, she was just happy that they were able to stop at the last minute.

This way of thinking seemed to be common among Christian leaders I knew. The general message I received from them was "Don't worry about being an uptight holiness freak! Just go out there and live a normal life! Watch the same movies, listen to the same music, go to the same parties, and do the same things everyone else does, but try not to do any of the really bad things—like premarital sex or drugs. And if you mess up every once in a while, hey, that's okay. God loves you anyway, and He will forgive you if you ask Him to." When it came to things like gossip, selfishness, dishonesty, laziness, arrogance, or even seductive behavior, these leaders didn't seem to have much to say. In fact, I often observed those very things in *their* lives on a regular basis. Even when something seemed harmless or when I saw other Christians doing it without any trace of guilt, if it did not reflect the nature of Jesus Christ, I had to train myself to walk away. It was not that I never sinned again—far from it! But sin no longer controlled my life. The more I learned to immediately flee from temptation, the more my sanctuary was protected, and the more amazing intimacy I discovered with my Prince.

Next I learned how to take the very first step on the road upward—developing a resistant attitude toward sin. Protecting my sanctuary was not only a defensive action; it was an offensive one as well. By determining on a daily basis that sin would not gain control over me, I was ready to employ the sudden-death technique when faced with temptation. Fleeing from temptation was not just something I did so that I could avoid sinning. It was a glorious step on the road upward—the road that would lead me to discover more and more of my Prince within my inner sanctuary. And with every success, I gained strength and momentum for the next.

PRACTICAL STEPS FOR RESISTING TEMPTATION

You are thinking that controlling your imagination does not depend on yourself...but it depends very much on yourself! When you cut off all the restless and unprofitable thoughts that you can control, you will greatly reduce all those thoughts which are involuntary. God will guard your imagination if you do your part in not encouraging your wayward thoughts.

FRANÇOIS FÉNELON

For many forms of temptation, fleeing is a *physical* act—like an alcoholic choosing to walk past a bar without pausing, or a young man choosing to immediately look away when a Victoria's Secret billboard suddenly screams for his attention. It's important to learn to recognize those forms of temptation in your own life and be ready to *physically* walk away, turn away, or look away when that moment of decision comes. But quite often, fleeing from temptation is not a physical act but a *mental* one. Think back to Clare's story. From the moment in the movie theater to her midnight musings, most of the temptation she faced took place inside her own mind.

Many of us struggle with constant thoughts of worthlessness, discontentment, resentment, or fear. Those kinds of thoughts are another form of temptation—the temptation to believe lies about ourselves, others, or our Prince. Martin Luther once wrote, "You can't stop the birds from flying over your head, but you can keep them from building a nest in your hair." We may not be able to keep the thoughts from entering our minds, but we can keep them from *staying* in our minds— by kicking them out the moment they arrive! Giving in to those thoughts and allowing them to linger in our heads allows them to take root inside our hearts and begin to control our lives. Remember that protecting our inner sanctuary is not just a defensive action; it requires playing offense as well. And one of the best offensive moves we can make is to set up a guard station at the entrance of our minds. Instead of passively allowing any and all random thoughts to saunter right on in and hang out for as long as they want, we must actively begin chasing away any thought that is not a reflection of our Prince, Jesus Christ.

Often an un-Christlike thought—whether it is a self-loathing thought of worthlessness, a burning hatred toward someone else, a paralyzing fear of the future, or a gnawing desire to experiment with sin—will be quite persistent in its attempt to occupy our minds. The moment we kick it out, it will be back at the door of our minds, pounding furiously, demanding that we let it come in and stay awhile. That's when it's time to pull out the really big guns!

BIG GUN #1: *Truth Serum.* Lies are destroyed by truth. When we are tempted to start believing lies about ourselves, others, or our Prince, it's time to fill our minds with so much truth that the lies will have no desire to come in and make themselves at home—in fact, they will be forced to run the other way! To fill our mind with truth, we must fill our minds with Scripture. At the moment of temptation, we can ignore the lie and instead dwell on the words of our Prince found in the Bible. It is not always practical to pull out a Bible at any time of the day or night; that's why *memorizing* Scripture is a wonderful tool for those intense moments of mental temptation.

Before your eyes glaze over at the very mention of Scripture memorization, let me assure you that it is not as difficult or tedious as it sounds, and anyone can learn how to do it! As important as it is to learn the words of Scripture, it is even more vital to dwell on the powerful, miraculous truth behind those words. As you fill your mind with Scripture, make a focused effort to dwell on how the words of your Prince should impact your life in a practical way.

Once we begin filling our minds with truth by memorizing the amazing, life-giving words of our Prince, we will wonder why we waited so long to begin. A great place to start is by memorizing some of the psalms. (Some of my favorites are Psalms 27, 32, 34, and 37.) Whenever we are faced with temptation, those words of truth can become vital weapons with which to chase away un-Christlike thoughts. The more we consistently fill our minds with truth, the scarcer lies will become.

BIG GUN #2: *Hitting Below the Belt.* Just as we have a very real Hero and Savior in our Prince, Jesus Christ, we also have a very real enemy, Satan. This enemy of ours wants nothing more than to destroy our inner sanctuary and pull us as far away from our Prince as possible. He hates us, and he hates Jesus Christ even more. Satan is aware of our personal weaknesses. Those are the areas he likes to pounce on, hoping that he can entice us to give in to temptation and eventually become controlled by sin. If we have struggled to remain content during times of loneliness or singleness, Satan will often try to oppress us with a shower of depression or despair. If we have experienced trauma or abuse in our past, Satan will often assault us with feelings of worthlessness or thoughts of bitterness toward the people who hurt us. If we have a weakness toward any kind of addiction (sexual, substance, or otherwise), Satan will often plant thoughts of longing for that fix at the door of our minds.

But we are not defenseless against his tactics. Our heroic Prince is on our side, and He is always victorious over our enemy. Our Prince has provided us with many weapons to use against our enemy, and one of the most effective of these weapons is prayer. I'm not talking about just praying defensively, asking our Prince to give us strength to flee from temptation. I'm also talking about praying *offensively*, asking that our Prince, in His amazing, heroic strength and power, would wreak havoc on the enemy of our souls. There is nothing Satan hates more than seeing a lost sinner come to know Jesus Christ. When our enemy is attacking us, one of the very best ways to hit him below the belt is to pray specifically for unsaved people in our lives to discover Jesus Christ.

One year before Eric and I were married, he and his sister worked together in a ministry position. Eric and Krissy made a powerful team, and it wasn't long before Satan began to take notice of the impact their unity was making on the lives of those they worked with. Soon they realized that the temptation to become irritated with each other over small issues was becoming a common occurrence. They recognized it as an attack from their enemy. They decided that whenever they were tempted to give in to frustration with each other, instead of yielding to the irritation, they would pray for the salvation of their neighbor, Charlie. Those unified prayers dissolved the tension between them, and it wasn't long before the attack on their relationship stopped altogether. They had hit their enemy where it hurts by using prayer as an offensive weapon. By the end of that year, Charlie had discovered Jesus Christ, and Eric and Krissy's relationship was stronger than ever.

We must identify the areas of our lives where we are most vulnerable to temptation. Do we struggle with depression? Do we have a weakness in the area of sexual temptation? Whenever Satan tries to pounce on our vulnerable areas, we can use those opportunities to hit him below the belt by praying for the salvation of someone we know who is in need of Jesus Christ. It is important that we develop this technique as a *habit* in our lives rather than just as a one-time attempt. When our enemy sees the consistency with which we use this tactic, he will back off in a hurry, and we just might get to see another life eternally changed in the process!

CREATING SOLID BOUNDARY LINES

Actress Portia Nelson captured her life story using just a few brief sentences in her famous poem "Autobiography in Five Short Chapters." In the first chapter, she is walking down the street and falls into a deep hole in the sidewalk. "It takes forever to find a way out," she says. In the next chapter, she walks down the same street, pretending she doesn't see the hole. She falls in again, and again struggles to get out. Eventually, she walks down the same street, managing to go around the hole. But the complete fifth chapter tells her ultimate solution: "I walk down another street.[17]

We all have our own personal holes in the sidewalk—areas of weakness that cause us to stumble and fall and lose ground in our relationship with our Prince. Most of us can relate to Portia Nelson's story. We see the hole, convince ourselves we can step over the hole, and end up falling in anyway. Or maybe we make a huge effort to avoid the hole, the whole time glancing over our shoulders, enticed by the hole and wishing we could walk just a little closer to it. Very few of us ever consider the fact that there is another option: *to take a different street.*

Nicole, a precocious college coed from Florida, has a different problem. "I want to wait faithfully for my future husband," she wrote in an e-mail, "but every time I watch romantic movies, it just makes me want to go out and get into a relationship right now! I get so impatient, and then I end up in these stupid, short-term relationships with guys who only want to use me."

Then there is Michelle, a soft-spoken computer whiz from Tennessee. "My life is so hectic I hardly have time to sleep," she told me not long ago. "Between school, work, sports, and friends, I start early in the morning and don't finish until the middle of the night. There's really nothing I can cut out of my life, but lately I've noticed I don't ever have time for prayer and Bible study. It's hard to grow spiritually when I'm this busy."

Andrea is a talented drama major at a college in Colorado. She has struggled with eating disorders for several years. "Every time I'm waiting in line at the grocery store or gas station, I start paging through the magazines at the check stand," she confided to me. "I see all these beautiful, thin models, and I start feeling fat and ugly. Then I go home and decide I'm not eating for a week."

All these young women keep falling into that hole in the sidewalk, time and time again, even though they try so carefully to step around it. Their struggles are very different, but the solution for each one of them is the same—*take a different street.* They need to put up a roadblock in front of that same old familiar street with the dangerous hole in the sidewalk. Developing eagle eyes toward sin, learning to flee from temptation, and discovering the secret of offensive prayer and Scripture memorization are all incredibly important ways of protecting our inner sanctuary. But there is another crucial aspect of protecting our sanctuary: adding practical, built-in, daily protections against compromise into our everyday lives. In essence, block off the wrong streets so we are free to walk down the right ones.

With the help of my Prince, I learned to become more aware of the areas in which I was prone to stumble. As I mentioned earlier, things like gossip, selfishness, laziness, self-pity, and materialism topped the list when it came to my tendency to compromise. I took a close look at my daily life—my habits, pastimes, friendships, and outside influences—and asked myself the question, *Is there anything in my life that is contributing to my tendency to compromise in these areas?* I was surprised at what I discovered. Some compromise triggers were fairly obvious: spending hours at the mall on weekends and poring through *Vogue* magazine definitely encouraged my materialistic tendencies. I created some practical boundaries around this area: I began to plan my weekends ahead of time so I wouldn't end up idly wandering through the aisles of the Gap every Saturday. And I stopped buying magazines that constantly screamed at me to acquire more and more.

Other compromise triggers were subtler. It took me a while, but eventually I realized that television had become a large contributing factor to my tendency toward a selfish attitude. All the characters on every show, however far from reality the story lines might be, were primarily focused only on themselves and their own needs, worries, or problems. Subconsciously, I had begun to believe that this kind of self-focused lifestyle was normal and acceptable, and in subtle ways I saw it come out in my everyday life. Then there were all the commercials convincing me to make my life better by doing this or getting that. All too often, I realized, I had begun to mirror the "look out for number one" attitude in my daily life.

I decided to create a boundary line in the area of television. I had never been a couch potato, but I had developed the habit of relaxing in front of a few sitcoms several nights a week or flipping through channels whenever I was bored. I had recently read the amazing true story of David Wilkerson, the founder of Teen Challenge and pastor of Times Square Church in New York City. He had been a simple country preacher in rural Pennsylvania. Every night for a couple of hours he would watch television, partially to relax and partially to stay in touch with the culture. One night a strange thought entered his mind: what if he were to get rid of his television and instead spend those two hours every night in prayer? To make a long story short, he tried it. He sold his television, got on his knees, and from that point forward, incredible things began happening in his life and ministry. David's life became an unprecedented adventure that impacted the lives of millions.[18]

His story inspired me to make a similar decision. I stopped watching television almost completely and started using my spare time to get to know my Prince in an even deeper way. It was a practical boundary I created, not because I believed that television was necessarily bad, but because I had seen the subtle, un-Christlike influence it had over my outlook and attitude, not to mention how it stole my valuable time. I had thought it would be a hard sacrifice to make, but soon I did not even miss it. I had so much more time for the things that were truly important, and gaining an unselfish outlook on life was easier when I stopped bonding with Jerry Seinfeld throughout my week.

Even now, many years after first learning how to protect my inner sanctuary, I have to actively and constantly work on keeping practical boundaries around my life. These days my compromise triggers don't come from magazines or television; they usually come in the form of busyness, phone calls, e-mail, and deadlines. In modern-day Christian ministry, Eric and I have discovered that it is all too easy to become so preoccupied with pointing others to Jesus Christ that we can easily forget to point *ourselves* to Him on a daily basis. About a year after our ministry began, our life became so frenzied that we realized we were in desperate need of boundaries around our lives to protect our marriage and our relationship with Jesus Christ.

The boundaries were simple, but the results were life changing. We set definite starting and stopping times for our work schedules so that we would not end up working into the night. We turned off the phones after hours, including our cell phones. We set aside certain times during our week to respond to our e-mail instead of replying every time we received a new message. We put restrictions on how many speaking engagements we would accept each year. We did not hold ministry-related meetings on weekends or during evenings. We set aside uninterrupted time every morning of the week for prayer, Bible study, and personal spiritual growth. We set aside time during each week for focusing on each other. When Eric and I respect these practical boundaries, they keep our priorities straight and our lives in balance in the midst of a chaotic world. The holes in the sidewalk are still there, waiting for us, but we have chosen to take a different street.

PRACTICAL STEPS FOR CREATING BOUNDARIES

Take a good, long look at your daily life—your habits, pastimes, friends, and outside influences. Ask yourself what holes in the side-walk you frequently fall into (or nearly fall into) on a regular basis. What are the practical boundaries you can create in your life so that you are free to take a different street? The compromise triggers in your life may not be wrong or sinful in and of themselves. But if any friendship, relationship, influence, or activity tends to draw you *away from Jesus Christ,* or keeps you from reflecting His lily-white likeness, that is the sign that a boundary line must be created in that area of your life.

Ask your Prince to show you what practical boundaries you need to create in your life so that you can protect your inner sanctuary. Remember that a boundary line you decide to create in your life might go against what you have always considered normal. For instance, there might be an expectation from your friends or co-workers that you are always reachable via e-mail, pager, or cell phone. But that doesn't mean you shouldn't consider putting limits on your availability to the outside world. Or you might feel strange going to bed earlier than everyone else just so that you can protect your morning quiet time with your Prince. But that doesn't mean you shouldn't do it anyway. Maybe no one in your life will understand your decision to set your life aside for your future husband. But don't let the irritated comments or uncomprehending stares of the world around you deter you from your goal. A lily does not try to resemble or imitate the thorns around her. She is focused on being who she was created to be—completely set apart for her heroic Lover.

A Picture of Set-Apartness
KOREA, 1939

Esther was a bright young Korean woman who had just begun her career as a music teacher at a Christian school when her life was forever changed in a single moment of decision. One morning as school began, a stern-looking woman approached her. Esther glanced up. It was the school principal. The principal told her that the Japanese authorities (who controlled Korea) were requiring students and teachers from all the schools in the area to travel to the shrine of Amaterasu Omikami, the sun goddess, in order to worship there. "Get your students ready—we must get there on time," said the woman in a firm voice. Esther's jaw tightened in defiance at the words. As a devoted follower of Christ, how could she ever agree to worship at the shrine of an idol? The very idea caused her stomach to turn.

The principal saw the rebellion in Esther's face and became

irritated. "You think you are the only Christian here?" she lashed out angrily. "You think you are the only one who does not want to bow to heathen gods? We all hate to do such a thing, but we are being persecuted by a power too ruthless to stand against. Unless we worship at the Japanese shrine, they will close this school!" Esther considered the principal's words. She saw the fear in the other woman's eyes. She understood the dilemma the school was in. The principal, along with many other Korean Christians in the city, felt that they had no choice but to go along with the Japanese authorities in order to protect themselves and their families from imprisonment, torture, and even death. But what about the words of Jesus Christ when He said, "I am the way, and the truth, and the life" (John 14:6)? How could these Christian leaders go directly against Him by compromising with idolatry?

The principal was still waiting for a reply. When Esther remained silent, the principal's face grew hard. "You can see how much trouble you will cause this school if you fail to cooperate," she said harshly, "but you don't seem to care about that. You are only thinking of yourself!"

Finally Esther spoke. "Okay—I will go to the shrine," she said quietly, moving toward the stairs.

The principal hurried after her. "And you will worship at the shrine too, right?" she questioned anxiously. Esther did not answer.

On the long trek to the shrine, with her students following silently behind her, Esther searched her heart. She knew when she arrived at the place of worship she would be forced to make a life-altering choice. She fixed her eyes on the vast sky beyond the hills and thought of Shadrach, Meshach, and Abed-nego, when they were commanded to bow to the statue of the Babylonian king, Nebuchadnezzar. The three young men had decided that even if God did not choose to save them from the burning fire, they would die honoring Him.

At that moment, Esther knew what she would do. Even though all the other Christians had decided that outwardly bowing to the idol was acceptable as long as they continued to worship Christ in their hearts, Esther could make no such compromise. She would not bow to any other but the one true God. Defying the Japanese warlords would most likely mean torture and imprisonment, but Esther decided that she would not live her youthful life for herself. She would offer it fully to her Prince, Jesus Christ. She said a silent prayer to Him. *Today on the mountain, before the large crowd, I will proclaim that there is no other god but You,* she declared.

Esther's group was the last to arrive at the shrine. A huge crowd had gathered, standing in straight, respectful lines, afraid to move because of the cruel gazes of the Japanese policemen. A few of the authorities eyed Esther and her students with disapproval as they joined the rest of the worshipers. Esther's heart began to pound with dread for what she was about to do. A sense of uneasiness swept over her, and she silently repeated the Lord's Prayer over and over. *Lord,* she prayed, *I am so weak! Please help me do this—watch over me as I stand for You.*

"Attention!" came the commanding voice of one of the officials. The crowd stood in silence and submission. "Our profoundest bow to Amaterasu Omikami!" As he shouted the words, the entire group bent the upper half of their bodies, bowing solemnly before the shrine. Esther was the only one who remained standing, looking up at the sky. The fear and uncertainty that had gripped her just moments before had vanished. Calmness and peace flooded her. She had done what her Prince had asked her to do. On the long walk back to the school, Esther continued her dialogue with her Master. *I have done what I should have done,* she prayed passionately. *Now, I commit the rest to You. I died today on that mountain—now it is only You who lives through me. I leave everything in Your hands.*

When Esther arrived back at the school, four detectives were waiting for her. Years of intense suffering for her Lord were about to begin. But something had happened to Esther that day in front of the shrine, something that changed her forever. She was no longer afraid of what men could do to her; her life was only a tool in the hands of her Lord. While others gave in to their fear, she had stood to protect what was most sacred in her life—her relationship with her Prince, Jesus Christ. It was a treasure she was determined to guard at all costs, even with her very life.

Esther was willing to be set apart from all the other young women in her generation by fearlessly protecting what was sacred. Her life was used incredibly by God as a result. She spent six harrowing years in Japanese prisons, changing the lives of both prisoners and guards by her amazing example of sacrificial love for her Prince. Her incredible story was published as a book in Korea and became an all-time religious bestseller there, igniting the spark of courage and hope in the hearts of countless Christians.[19]

Today, examples of young women who sacrifice their safety, comfort, and very lives to protect the truth of Jesus Christ are rare. Most Christian young women in today's culture balk at the thought of truly *living* set-apart lives for their Prince, let alone *dying* for Him. But in every generation, there are a few who make another choice—a choice to heroically guard their sacred relationship with their Prince, no matter what the cost. Are you willing to be one of the few?

CHAPTER EIGHT IN A NUTSHELL

Our sacred, inner sanctuary, though it is a holy chamber of unparalleled peace and rest, is a marked target for daily enemy ambush. As set-apart young women, we must condition ourselves to be watchful to the subtle maneuverings of our enemy. Our enemy studies us and learns our weaknesses; he is crafty and devilishly sly. Temptation is one of his malevolent weapons that he has wielded like a battle-ax throughout the centuries. He knows that if he can catch us off our guard, it can provide him with the license to destroy. If we don't aggressively slam the door of our souls when he knocks, he will slither into our most sacred places and plant seeds of spiritual decay within our souls.

But our Prince trains us, as His set-apart ones, not to live our spiritual lives on the defensive. Rather, He instructs us how to live with spiritual aggressiveness and how to go on the offensive in our spiritual posture. We may have an enemy bent on destroying us, but we can learn to take everything our enemy could use to harm us and allow our Prince to transform it into greater spiritual depth and strength. As set-apart young women, everything that bombards our lives can be an opportunity for a greater imprint of Christ upon our souls. This battle is found in every moment, with every choice, and with every inclination of the heart. If we learn to take these moments, yield to our Prince, and slam the door on our enemy, what glorious possibilities for growth await us each and every day!

9

Feminine Mystique
and Romance

Future Husband Application

*The unmarried young woman centers her earthly existence around
the affairs of her heavenly Prince, and her aim in life is to be
completely set apart for Him, in body and in spirit.*

1 CORINTHIANS 7:34, PARAPHRASE[20]

DANIELLE IS a friendly, green-eyed,
red-headed eighteen-year-old from Oregon. She has been raised in a
Christian home and is a leader in her church youth group. She has
never been in a relationship. She's never even been kissed. She is
incredibly frustrated by this. She recently vented some of her emotions to me via e-mail. "No one these days has *never* been kissed!" she
writes in disgust. "What am I doing? Living in the Dark Ages?"
Danielle confided to me that she doesn't believe that saving herself
will be much of an appeal to any guy in today's world. *Who would*

151

want a girl who has never been kissed, never even had a boyfriend? she wonders every night as she lies in bed. "Guys will probably just assume that I am a second-rate choice that no one has ever wanted," she writes, her words overflowing with despair. Danielle is ready to jump into a fling with the first available guy she meets to prove to the world that she is not a relational reject.

Casey is a young college graduate with similar concerns. From an early age she made the decision to save herself for her future husband, but now she is flooded with doubt about her choice. "My parents and friends always tell me to get out there and find someone before it is too late and to quit waiting around for a perfect Christian guy!" she told me in frustration. "Now they are saying I should go hang out at bars and clubs just so I can meet guys!" she added, shaking her head in confusion. "And there are men in my life who tell me that a girl who is twenty-five and still a virgin is not something that *any* man will see as a gift!" Casey is tempted to scrap her commitment to purity to prove to her family and friends that she isn't holding out for a ridiculous, unrealistic ideal.

How does feminine mystique fit into a world that holds nothing sacred? How does a young woman jealously guard her heart and body as a treasure for her future husband when nearly all the men in today's world go out of their way to convince her that such a treasure is worthless? I could encourage Danielle and Casey with a predictable Christian response to their despair: "Don't worry. Someday you'll find a man who will be so happy that you never gave yourself to anyone else. Your future husband will totally appreciate the sacrifices you are making for him." That kind of statement has a lot of truth to it. If God's plan for a young woman's life is marriage, and if she is willing to wait for His perfect timing, He will bring into her life a man who reflects *His* character—a man who will see her purity as an incredible treasure.

SOMETHING WORTH WAITING FOR

Feminine mystique is not a begrudging commitment to physical or emotional purity. Feminine mystique is not developed through doubt-filled, lonely nights of self-pity, wondering if anyone will ever be attracted to us. Feminine mystique is not legalistic hypermodesty, hiding our womanhood behind long, shapeless robes and veils. Feminine mystique is the steady, unyielding strength and confidence that flows from knowing our Prince intimately and protecting our relationship with Him at all costs.

A young woman with feminine mystique does not protect her inner sanctuary on the condition that she will one day find a man who will appreciate it. She does not ask, "Is this sacrifice really worth it?" Instead, a young woman with feminine mystique—who jealously guards her heart, mind, and body from the pollution of the world—does so as a natural outflow of her passionate love for her true Prince.

The number-one question I get asked by young women is this: "Are there really any guys out there who are worth waiting for?" Observing typical guy behavior in today's culture can be overwhelmingly discouraging! You may be one of the countless young women who have wondered this very question time and time again. But before I deal with that issue, let me ask *you* a much more important question: "Are you willing to keep your inner sanctuary sacred and live a set-apart life out of love for your Prince, even if you *never* find a man who is worth waiting for?" As I mentioned in the beginning of this book, my love story with Eric is only a *small* reflection of the far more amazing love story I have discovered with my true Prince, Jesus Christ. And even if I had never met Eric, never had a beautiful love story with him, never gotten married at all, living a set-apart life for my Prince alone would be so much more than worth it.

Until a young woman develops the attitude that everything she does is for her Prince alone, she cannot develop the art of true feminine mystique. Before reading any further in this section, I urge you to search your heart and ask yourself this question: *Am I willing to remain set apart for my Prince alone, no matter what happens in my future?* When our Prince becomes the core reason behind every decision we make, unshakable confidence and strength will begin to flow into our lives.

THE MODERN-DAY JERK EPIDEMIC

And now, back to that ever-popular question: *Are* there really any guys out there worth waiting for? Are there really guys today who see a set-apart, lily-white young woman as a valuable treasure? Those questions are valid. Today's men seem more attracted to young women like Tanya, the girl from my high school who was so comfortable with her body that she let a crowd gather while she had sex with her boyfriend. Even Christian guys seem to pay more attention to the girls who tirelessly flirt, shamelessly flaunt their bodies, and make themselves overtly available for short-term relationships.

When I was young, my parents would exhort me with statements like "Men don't like women who are too aggressive. You shouldn't be the one to call a guy; you should let *him* call you. You shouldn't be the one to initiate a relationship; you should let *him* be the one to tell you he's interested." But by the time I reached middle school, I had become convinced that this kind of advice was grossly outdated. The girls who were popular among the guys were never the ones sitting quietly in the background, shyly waiting for guys to come to them. The girls who got all the male attention were the ones who put all their time, effort, and flirtatious energy into getting the guys they wanted. The guys did not seem to be turned off by this in-your-face approach; they seemed to actually like it! One day in seventh grade, Aaron, the curly-haired basketball player whose locker was next to mine, handed me a small scrap of notebook paper. "Here's my phone number," he said with a sly wink. "Call me, okay?" According to my parents, boys didn't like it when girls called them, but here was a guy *asking* me to call him and giving me his number. Whatever version of boys my parents were referring to, I decided, must have gone extinct along with *Tyrannosaurus rex*.

The mistake that too many of us make is that we *give in* to the attitude of men in the culture and allow our feminine mystique to be trampled in the mud. In high school, it didn't take me long to learn the trick of giggling while guys explored my body in the halls or whispered perverted comments in my ear on the bus and during classes. This kind of occurrence only became more and more common as I got older. I had no desire to be like the reclusive, prudish young women who got upset when guys treated them like sex objects. Those girls, it was rumored, had "issues"—they were presumably either not comfortable with their bodies or were afraid of sex, and as a result they got nothing but cruel disdain from both guys *and* girls.

And so my romantic flings held little mystique at all. When I was fourteen, Brandon, my first "serious" boyfriend, introduced me to this concept on our first official date. It took place at a party in my friend Brook's basement. The other partygoers just happened to be six other couples, and I quickly learned that the purpose of the get-together was not to sit around and chat and eat popcorn or listen to music—it was to pair off with our significant others in various corners and make out for the majority of the evening. As Brandon led me to a remote spot of the basement, I felt a quick stab of guilt, knowing my parents would definitely not approve of this kind of party. But what was I supposed to do? Leave? Make a scene? Be the only girl there who was prudish enough to object? It was not even an option in my mind.

By the end of the night, my clothes were wrinkled, my hair was disheveled, and I smelled strongly of Polo, Brandon's signature scent. I stood in Brook's bathroom gazing guiltily at myself in the mirror, overcome with embarrassment, trying in vain to smooth out the incriminating evidence of that night's activities. But at that moment, the door swung open. Kelly and Stacy—two popular cheerleaders who had also been at the party—stood there looking at my extremely ruffled appearance. With an excited squeal, Kelly rushed over to me. "Oh my gosh! You and Brandon were really going at it!" she giggled in delight, motioning Stacy to come and see for herself.

By the time school started the next day, my popularity level had soared. My first class was computer lab, and as soon as the teacher left us to work on a programming assignment, two of Brandon's buddies slid over to my chair with sly grins on their faces.

"Heard you and Brandon got *busy* last night," said one, giving me a knowing wink.

"Yeah, he's a lucky guy," the other declared, looking me up and down. "When you two break up, let me know, okay?"

I was surprised by the newfound approval my make-out session with Brandon had gained me. It didn't take long to discover that the less I held back, and the less cautious or embarrassed I was, the more accepted I would be. And so I threw nearly all my feminine mystique out the window. I learned to shamelessly flirt with guys and engage in casual sexual banter, show off my body with tight, seductive clothes, jump into casual dating relationships, and give myself physically and emotionally to guy after guy—then brag to my friends about it. As I grew up, I allowed the jerk epidemic in my world to completely dictate the way I acted, spoke, and dressed around guys.

I heard recently of a middle school that sent a letter to all the parents to address a problem that the school administration referred to as an "epidemic of oral sex" among the students. A huge number of the sixth- through eighth-grade girls were performing oral sex for their male classmates on a regular basis—in classrooms, in the halls, on the campus grounds, and in the bathrooms, not to mention at parties on the weekends. This is not a problem unique to just one middle school, however. I have heard from several young girls around the country about this new sexual trend.

"It's not the same as sex," was the confident statement from Wendy, a misguided thirteen-year-old softball player during a candid discussion about the issue. "It's a much better way for girls to give the guys what they want without having to get pregnant or get an STD."

"Guys don't even have to ask for it anymore," added Alyssa, Wendy's twelve-year-old friend. "Girls just do it automatically—even to guys they don't know. That's the way a girl can be accepted by everyone."

Our world today is a far cry from the olden days of romantic mystique, when gallant, chivalrous men actually *protected* the sacred innocence of women. But does that mean we should toss feminine mystique to the wind without a second thought?

When I first met my Prince and created my inner sanctuary, I had to be completely rebuilt when it came to relating to the opposite sex. Since my interaction with nearly every guy in my life was centered on flirting and sexual banter, it was hard to maintain feminine mystique even in casual friendships with guys. I hadn't realized how much I relied on flirtatious interaction with guys to prove to myself and to the world that I could be attractive to the opposite sex. Deliberately stopping that kind of banter made me feel isolated and insecure. But each time I was tempted to fall back into my old habits, I pressed in even closer to my Prince. He tenderly reminded me that I was His lily among thorns and that the typical ways of other young women were unfitting for me, His set-apart princess.

My Prince showed me more ways to guard my feminine

mystique. I began to be careful about the way I dressed around guys. I began to be careful about the way I spoke to guys. I began to be careful about how much I shared with guys. I began to be careful about how much time I spent with guys. I began to be careful not to open my heart to guys.

An amazing thing happened when I finally learned to protect my femininity instead of tossing it to the wind. For the first time ever, I began to meet young men who actually *valued* and *protected* feminine mystique. I hadn't even realized guys like this existed. I was shocked that, suddenly, I started to come in contact with a whole new breed of men. But looking back, it makes sense. Why would someone with higher standards take any notice of me when I had been spending all my energy proving to the world that I was just like every other careless young woman out there, throwing my heart, mind, and body to guy after guy? But when I began to guard my femininity and live differently than the other young women of the culture, guys who were committed to living differently started to appear in my life.

I did not see these guys as potential relationships, but as true friends and brothers in Christ. They treated me with complete respect and dignity. Our interactions were not based on the casual flirting I had always had with other guys. Our friendships were centered on Jesus Christ. They did not try to draw me to themselves; they did not try to tempt me to give them pieces of my heart or body. Instead, they encouraged me in my pursuit of my Prince.

If you are still asking that perplexing question, "Are there any guys out there worth waiting for?" let me assure you—in the midst of our huge jerk epidemic, modern-day knights truly *do* exist! Granted, they are few and far between. But after spending several years traveling this country and other countries and interacting with countless young adults, I have been truly amazed at some of the heroic, Christlike Warrior Poets who are out there.

"But I never see *any* guys like that!" you may protest. The reason for this is probably because Christlike Warrior Poets aren't usually mixed in with all the other jerks. They are living set-apart lives, just as our Prince has called us to do. They aren't often found in the normal crowds at typical guy-girl hangouts. They don't typically seek the spotlight. They aren't in hot pursuit of girls; they don't try to satisfy their loneliness with relationships. Christlike Warrior Poets can often be found on their knees in hidden retreats with their King, or on the battlefield of human service, or in diligent study of their Lord's ways.

Even if you do not see any Christlike Warrior Poets in your life, do not lower your standards and settle for less in a guy. Your heavenly Prince is more than capable of bringing your Warrior Poet into your life in His own perfect way, if His plan and purpose for you is marriage.

Young women often ask me what they should look for in a man. I tell them to settle for nothing less than a man who reflects the very attitude and character of their Prince, Jesus Christ. Our Prince protects and honors our femininity, and so will a Christlike man. To a Christlike Warrior Poet, feminine mystique is not something to be conquered or mocked; it is a beautiful, fascinating quality to be valued and cherished forever. Even if a young woman longs for human companionship and loathes the idea of singleness, I still believe it is better for her to remain single than to settle for anything less. When it comes to relationships, let this be your goal: to protect your feminine mystique at all costs and wait for a man who will guard your sacred treasure with his life.

TESTING TRUE LOVE

"But how will I know when a relationship *is* right?" chorus the many women who are still waiting for a God-written love story. Here is a

---

great litmus test for any relationship in our lives—friendship or otherwise. As we examine the influence the relationship has over us, we must ask ourselves these questions: *Does this person help me protect my inner sanctuary? Does this relationship draw me closer to my Prince?*

Shortly before my love story with Eric began, he and my dad met together one morning at Perkins Restaurant. It was a memorable conversation, which greatly affected my relationship with Eric before it even started. My dad told Eric many things that day, but one statement in particular stood out: "I know that your friendship with Leslie is from God," my dad said, "because ever since you have been in her life, she has drawn closer to Jesus Christ."

Later, when I pondered those words, I was amazed at how true they were. Since the very first day I had met Eric Ludy, he had done nothing but inspire me to pursue more and more of my true Prince. He lived a life of passionate abandonment to his Lord. Following after Jesus Christ with all his heart, soul, mind, and strength seemed to be his sole preoccupation in life. Whenever I was around him, his spiritual fire seemed to ignite my own, and after being with him I would usually end up on my knees poring over my Bible, digesting all the new thoughts and insights he had inspired within me. Throughout our friendship, Eric had never attempted to draw my attention to himself but always pointed me back to my true Prince, Jesus Christ. He actively helped me protect my inner sanctuary.

Even after our romance officially began, he continued to lead me right back into the arms of my Prince. As excited as I was about having Eric in my life, I learned not to lean on this newly discovered human love for my fulfillment and security. Though God had so faithfully blessed me with a beautiful human love story, it was still in my inner sanctuary of intimacy with Him that I found my reason to live. Even now, after years of marriage, Eric's primary goal is to lead me closer and closer to Christ every day we are together. He continues to help me protect the most sacred part of who I am—my inner sanctuary of intimacy with my true Prince.

Every stage of a love story that is truly initiated by our Prince—both the friendship and the romance—only *enhances* our intimacy with Him. If a relationship is not leading us closer and closer to Him, it will quickly become just another one of the other lovers cluttering up our sanctuary. Sadly, too many of us begin to build an inner sanctuary for our Prince and then get thrown completely off course because of a romantic relationship. A romantic relationship might very well have been initiated by God, but the moment our focus moves from our Prince to a human love story is the moment we cease to guard our sanctuary, and our entire foundation for success crumbles into ashes. A relationship that leads us *closer* to our Prince and carefully *protects* our inner sanctuary is the key to discovering romance as it was truly intended to be—a little taste of heaven on earth.

PRACTICAL STEPS FOR GUARDING FEMININE MYSTIQUE

Take a closer look at your life and ask yourself the following questions:

- Have I allowed the culture to convince me that my feminine mystique is worthless?
- Have I given away pieces of my heart, mind, emotions, or body, or even performed sexual favors to receive the approval of guys?
- Have I adopted the careless attitude of today's young women—encouraging the sexual attention of guys around me by the way I act or dress?
- Have I settled for less than a Christlike guy because I don't truly believe my Prince can bring anyone better into my life in His perfect time and way?

As your Prince gently points to different areas of your life in which you have allowed your feminine mystique to be compromised or destroyed, it is a good idea to write them down. Ask God to forgive you and wash you completely clean from those sins. Then, prayerfully think about some practical steps you can take to start protecting the sacred parts of who you are.

Guarding feminine mystique takes focused effort and time. One of the most practical ways to begin guarding our hearts is to turn off the incessant voice of the culture, which is shouting out messages that tempt us to second-guess our commitment to our Prince and a future husband. Sometimes we become so used to cultural influences that we don't even notice how they are affecting our attitudes toward feminine mystique. Movies, television, magazines, billboards, clothing ads, shampoo commercials, books, music, teachers, and friends—these are just a few of the most common ways the culture tries to get us to buy into the idea that feminine mystery is old-fashioned. They try to convince us that the "hold nothing back" approach is a much better way for a woman to live. We must carefully examine the influences in our life. Here are some more great soul-searching questions to ask:

- Are there voices I need to start ignoring?
- Are there shows or movies I need to stop watching?
- Are there places I need to stop going?
- Are there people I need to stop spending time with?
- Are there certain clothes I need to stop wearing?
- Are there songs I need to stop listening to?

Remember not to limit your examination to only secular influences in your life. A shocking disregard for feminine mystique has, sadly, crept into many modern-day Christian circles as well. When I attended different youth groups in high school, it seemed that every week the cute youth pastor would start his lesson with the presumption that all of us were completely consumed with the opposite sex.

"Okay, so what should you do when you're out with someone really hot this Friday night," he would say, "and he wants you to take a little tumble with him in the backseat of the car?"

If any of us openly lived according to different standards (like not pursuing a hot date every Friday night), the youth pastor would usually write us off as abnormal teenagers who needed to get a clue and then basically ignore us from that point on. Certainly not all youth leaders today have this attitude; thankfully there are those who greatly encourage set-apartness. And yet in many of today's churches, a subtle disdain for guarding what is sacred has crept in. Unfortunately, this is not limited only to the high-school level.

Not long ago I spoke with a young woman attending a well-known Christian college. "If you are not paired up with someone," she told me in frustration, "everyone here acts like there is something wrong with you—even the faculty. They are more concerned about your behavior if you are *single* than if you are *sleeping around*!"

Two young women recently told me they were concerned about the atmosphere being created in the megachurch they were attending—a high-powered weeknight gathering for twenty-somethings. "It seems to mostly be a meat market for Christian guys and girls to check each other out," one girl observed. "I really like the worship and the messages, but I feel like guys are checking me out the whole time!" added the other.

A bubbly twenty-year-old from California once told me she was confused about how to decide on which clothes were okay for her to wear and which weren't. "I used to try to be really careful about how tight my shirts were or how short my skirts were," she confided to me, "but I go to church and see all the other girls wearing really short, tight clothes, and nobody seems to care. And then I go to concerts and see Christian singers that I respect wearing that kind of stuff too, so now I wonder if I was just being overly paranoid about it."

As we seek to jealously protect our feminine mystique—from our hearts, to our minds, to our bodies—we must be aware that even certain Christian influences in our lives might need to be questioned and even eliminated. In my own life, I came to the point of realizing that most of the Christian gatherings targeting my age group were not usually leading me closer to my Prince—they were only presenting me with more opportunities to compromise my inner sanctuary. Let me emphasize that there are *plenty* of exceptions to this—I am simply sharing *my own* experience! I decided to spend my time participating in church services and Christian groups that were geared for every age and focused completely on Jesus Christ rather than groups that focused on the angst of the younger generation. And ironically, it was in these new Christ-centered, multiage environments that I eventually became friends with several young people my age who were truly building their lives around Christ and encouraging me to do the same.

When I say that we must remove any friendship, relationship, or influence in our lives that *pulls us away* from our commitment to guard our inner sanctuary and protect our feminine mystique, I do not mean we must live in isolation from the world around us. We are not just called to be lilies—but lilies *among the thorns,* reflecting the likeness of our Prince in the midst of a perverse generation. But there is a marked difference between a lily and the thorns that surround the lily. It is not from being *around* un-Christlike people or influences that our sanctuary is compromised; it is from *allowing* those un-Christlike people or influences to affect how we act or think. When we begin to sense that we are losing the lily-white likeness of our Prince and beginning to think or act more like the thorns around us, that's when it's time to change the scenery in our lives in order to protect our sacred sanctuary.

I once heard a youth leader talking about a conversation he had with a beautiful young woman who had come to him for advice. The girl was dating a good-looking athlete and was extremely attached to the relationship. But her boyfriend had begun to pressure her to do things she wasn't comfortable with—he wanted her to wear revealing outfits; he wrote her notes describing what he liked about her body; he even began to try to entice her physically when they were together. She didn't want to lose the relationship, but she felt that he was tempting her to compromise her heart and body.

At that point, she came to the youth leader for advice. The leader told her to stand firm in the commitments she had made and to tell her boyfriend that she wasn't comfortable with what he was suggesting. "He'll back down. You'll see," the leader reassured her. So the girl took his advice, stood up to her boyfriend, and managed to stay in the relationship for another year without compromising. Then they broke up and went their own ways. The girl was still a virgin when she got married a few years later. Sounds like a great story, right? At first glance it would seem that the girl had been successful in guarding her feminine mystique. But this young woman could have had so much more.

Feminine mystique is not a matter of clinging to a remnant of sacredness in the midst of a relationship with someone who has no respect for it. Remember, feminine mystique can only flow from a carefully guarded, jealously protected inner sanctuary of intimacy with our Prince. If a friendship or relationship does not enhance our inner sanctuary and respect and serve our feminine mystique, it does not belong in our lives. We must be willing to do whatever it takes— *no matter what the cost*—to protect our sacred sanctuary within.

CHAPTER NINE IN A NUTSHELL

Prince Charmings really do exist in this world. They are men who reflect our Prince Charming in heaven—Jesus Christ. As set-apart young women, our standards for earthly lovers must be calibrated to fit with the nature and character of our heavenly Lover. We must allow Him to train our eyes to see the beauty and strength of the internal life. We must learn to recognize and applaud integrity, selfless love, courage, compassion, and an intimate relationship with Christ. And when we do, we will be satisfied with nothing less than men who reflect the princely grace of our Jesus. We will recognize these men of God's choosing because they will have been shaped by our Prince. They will be set apart for the Prince's service, just as we are.

The Making of Warriors

by Eric Ludy

At the risk of exposing my fellow generation of guys to some uncomfortable scrutiny, I would like to pose a question not often uttered by a member of the male species: do guys today know what it takes to win a young woman's heart?

When I posed this question on a college campus recently, a red-headed girl with boysenberry nail polish retorted, "They have no clue!" while a blue-eyed sorority sister muttered sarcastically, "Uh, yeah, right!"

Well, let's quiz some guys and see how they would answer that question.

Chad, a WrestleMania fanatic with a nose ring and perfect attendance at his church's youth group, cautiously replied, "What are you going to use this for?" When he found out that his reply might end up in a book, he took his time. After a few weighty moments he finally stuttered, "Uh, I don't know!" He scratched his arm really hard like he had a sudden attack of the chicken pox, then said, "I guess they like things like flowers and stuff."

Ellis, a supertall, superthin, Afro-laden drummer, didn't take the same amount of time before he pronounced his opinion on the matter: "I think girls like a little attitude, a cocky kind of guy."

A husky nineteen-year-old, nicknamed Bubba, offered the most interesting response. Bubba sported a shaved head and baggy jeans and gnawed on a piece of gum (Hubba Bubba?) as if his life depended on it. He exclaimed, "Girls don't have a clue what they want, man!" He gave a couple gigantic cowlike movements of his jaw on the worn-out piece of gum, then added, with a noticeable hint of irritation in his voice, "They are totally confused!"

As a man, I can easily climb into Bubba's world. I have felt Bubba's irritation. And, just like Bubba, I have been totally upside-down in my perception of femininity. Unfortunately, our gum-smacking friend is in for a rude awakening. Many a well-meaning man has gotten caught in the "women are totally confused" trap throughout the centuries. But the truth is, *women really do know what they want.* So why do women today come across as so confused in their desires? If they really know what they want, why don't they tell us guys? There are two huge reasons:

1. As Leslie says, "Young women today are faced with a version of manhood that is so far beneath their ideal that they begin to feel that their expectations are probably unrealistic, their standard for male behavior is too high and probably too good to be true." We as humans tend to protect ourselves from disappointment. And today's young woman is no different. It's far more emotionally friendly for a young woman to squash her desires in the here and now than it is to keep her dreams alive and be crippled emotionally by the disappointment of them not coming true. But even the woman who attempts to squash these desires within cannot eliminate them from her heart. Thus we find the confused modern woman—in one moment desiring men to be Warrior Poets while in the next moment denying the fact that she ever expected men to be anything other than burpers and scratchers.

2. The second reason is, as my college buddy Sean used to bemoan, "A girl thing." Leslie again says it best: "We as girls tend to assume that men should know what we want with-

out our having to tell them. In fact, we go so far as to assume that, since a man doesn't seem to have even the remotest clue of our unspoken wants, he doesn't really care." In our marriage, when Leslie realized that my lack of knowing her wants wasn't a lack of caring but rather a lack of our communicating with each other about who she was and how she worked, our marriage intimacy skyrocketed. If a guy never understands a woman's heart, he will never know how to win it, protect it, and cherish it. Only a woman can teach him that. If you, as a young woman, remain silent, the best we as guys can do is guess.

Men have been taught that we will never figure women out, no matter now hard we try. That is an extremely dangerous lie. It is true that God-designed femininity should always hold a certain mystery to men, but men *can* learn how to understand a woman and nurture her heart. It isn't just important for you, as a young woman, that guys discover what wins your heart. It's crucial to our success as men—whether we ever get married or not.

Encrypted within the amazing design of authentic femininity is a golden key. It's a key that unlocks for us the mysteries of relational success with family, friends, a future bride, and most importantly, with Christ.

TWO MISSING INGREDIENTS

My dad said it well when he told me, "Eric, become a student of your wife and you will know what it means to be a man." Manhood, in its most polished form, is the perfectly built advocate of blossoming and radiant womanhood. When men become true men, they set women free to be everything that God intended them to be rather than oppressing femininity through their own selfishness.

In this study on manhood and in the one after chapter 12, I would like to explore how you can help men discover two all-important aspects of Christlike masculinity:

1. *How to be a warrior.* A warrior is more than just a defender of truth and justice and a champion for the weak. A warrior is also one trained to protect what is sacred and innocent within a woman.

2. *How to be a poet.* I'm not talking about being just a bearer of roses, rings, and rhymes. A true poet is trained to understand the intimate and sacred sanctuary of a woman's heart and to cultivate the same intimacy with Christ in his own heart.

Both of these qualities are important to the complete man. In this study let's focus on the first of the two qualities: how young men can be made into warriors.

THE MAKING OF WARRIORS

Just as young girls dream of becoming princesses, young boys dream of becoming warriors. When I was eleven I used to spend my time imagining how I could rescue my school if it were to be taken over by bad guys. I had a rather intricate scheme that I cooked up over a couple months' of, ahem, "doing my homework."

My strategy was to somehow escape from the screaming, puberty-stricken crowd and crawl up into the rafters of the gymnasium (it seemed logical to me that the bad guys would have herded us like cattle into the gym). I would carefully make my way through the rafters like a lion-hearted monkey until I was just above the head of the lead bad guy. Cindy McFarland would look up and notice me, and I would delicately place my finger in front of my mouth as if to say, "Shh, be very quiet; your hero has arrived!" Then, while the entire student body looked on in wonder, I would fly down from the rafters, knocking the lead bad guy senseless, and then with a few Karate Kid–like kicks (I imagined that I knew karate too), I would take out the other bad guys. The entire student body would erupt with applause and carry me out (on their shoulders, of course) to meet the television news anchors. In the end, Cindy McFarland would rush to my side and sigh, the way only a heroine can, "Eric Ludy, you are my hero!"

As men, the desire to be warriors is woven deep into the fabric of our beings. So why don't more of us grow up to be warriors? Well, for the same reason so many young men who want to drive a golf ball like Tiger Woods never become world-champion golfers. The raw material may be there (okay, maybe not enough material to become the next Tiger Woods), but we need more than that. We are given everything to make us into warriors except for one important ingredient: *basic training*.

Growing up, guys are given a training ground, a personal practice field on which we can be crafted into soldiers of honor. Most of us never realize that the obstacle courses of our younger years are intended by God to prepare us for future heroism. As young boys, we think that we need a bloody battlefield, a bomb to diffuse, or a bad guy in the school gymnasium to arouse the warrior within. But the truth is, if we don't learn to arouse the warrior within during our personal practice seasons, we will run like cowards when the battles, the bombs, and the bad guys appear.

This training ground looks different for each young man, but the essential exercise equipment by which he develops his courage "muscles" is basically the same. There are four categories of this basic training:

1. *Standing up for the little people*. The mercy and compassion "muscles" within a young man's heart are built when he learns to protect those who can't protect themselves (like the kid getting picked on). To the degree a young man allows

the Spirit of God to sculpt within him these muscles of compassion and justice, he will heroically shape the world.

2. *Befriending the outcasts.* To offer love rather than disdain to those considered untouchables is a level of Christlike nobility reached by few in this current generation.

3. *Protecting mothers and sisters.* A soldier's valor is directly proportional to how he protects and honors his women back home. How a young man trains as a protector within his family is the model of how he will act as a protector of his future wife and daughters as well as womanhood around him.

4. *Defending innocence.* A true warrior guards his own heart for intimacy with Christ and for the enjoyment of his future spouse. But beyond that, he also protects the purity and innocence of all young women. If a young man learns to forgo what would bring him short-term pleasure for what would honor and protect the sacredness of marriage, he is formidably prepared to protect the truth of the gospel. This is truly a lost art in the modern training of young men. We as guys have been taught to conquer rather than protect the innocent. "Dude, was she a virgin?" was the question posed, seemingly daily, in the guys' locker room to all the boasting "conquerors." Not only has this warped male-mentality impaired men romantically, it has crippled us spiritually. Since the male psyche has lost the value of the innocent, we don't recognize the importance of protecting the innocent within our own lives. The sanctuary of so many young, Christ-fearing men today is void of intimacy and overrun with sin simply because young men haven't been taught the value of protecting what is innocent.

PROTECTING EMOTIONAL NEEDS

When it comes to romance blunders, even in very healthy, God-fearing relationships, there is one blunder that Leslie and I see as often as the sunrise—and it's an issue that exposes the lack of trained warriors today.

Men, for the most part, are clueless when it comes to a feminine heart's true needs. Rather than being willing to diligently and respectfully win a girl's heart over time by listening to her, learning about her, doing thoughtful things for her, and making sure she is truly ready before moving to the next level, men tend to breeze right past the emotional wooing stage as if it is totally unnecessary.

Nowhere is this better illustrated than in marriages across this country. Married women know that the time it takes to make love is an entire day (to prepare her heart, to warm her heart, and then be ready to pour out her heart). Married men, on the other hand, would tell you that it takes five minutes (that's probably why many of them aren't making love very long after their honeymoons are over). A woman's heart is warmed slowly, and her physical senses are charmed over time, while a man can be instantly aroused physically and emotionally. When men use their own emotions and physical desires as the gauge for the progress of a relationship, they are usually met with a strange hesitation.

"Yeah! What's up with that?" screams nearly every guy I've ever talked with about romantic relationships. From a modern guy's vantage point, we don't realize that there is any difference between men and women except for those key biological differences, which we assume were spurred on by some weird thing called estrogen. Men don't know how to protect a woman's heart because they don't realize it is so different from their own. This is another area in which women can help us become warriors—men who guard and defend what is vulnerable.

Manhood is at its best when it can make a woman feel both protected in her innocence and secure in the slow warming of her heart. It's all a part of becoming the warriors God calls men to be.

PUTTING IT INTO ACTION

So let's get practical. Though you, as a young woman, are not the only tool that God uses to shape us as men, you are certainly one of the most important. You are a divinely positioned map in our lives to help us discover how to get to the city of Great Manhood. But since men don't like to admit that they are ever lost, and would often rather be stuck in the middle of Kansas for days than have to consult a map, how can you, as a young woman, help get us to look at your map? Let's look at four ways that a young woman can be more effective as a mapbearer for the up-and-coming warriors in her life:

1. *Be an inspiration.* Live out the kind of womanhood that inspires a man to protect. Knights in shining armor are made, in large part, by beholding fair maidens. When a man encounters the rare beauty of a set-apart young woman, he is inspired to defend what makes her beautiful and what is sacred at the core of her being.

2. *Be a talker.* A man can only understand a woman when a woman helps him understand her. While this is absolutely critical in marriage, it is also important for all other types of male-female relationships. And dads and brothers are a great practice ground. Take your dad and brothers through an introductory course in understanding who you are and how you work. To do this, you will need to start communicating. When you feel one of them is being insensitive, gently let

them know. When you feel you just need to be comforted by your dad, sweetly ask him to comfort you. When one of them is trying to solve your problem rather than just listen to you, tell him that you are not looking to get your problem fixed, but that you just need him to try to understand and simply validate your feelings. Then when Mr. Right strolls into your life, you will already be practiced up. Only when a man *knows* can a man respond.

3. *Be rescuable.* Men today have lost their sense of valor mainly because they lack the opportunities to cultivate it. So often today, women feel threatened by men who desire to help them. "I'm a woman! I can do it myself!" is the marching cry of the modern feminist regime. Just as men come across as pretty stupid for trying to make it to the city of Great Manhood without a map, women will never arrive at their destination, either, if they are unwilling to read the map that God has given them—*manhood.* Men stopped opening doors for women when they started getting slapped for doing it; they stopped laying their coats over mud puddles when they were accused of being chauvinistic as a result. But those simple means of expressing honor and value to women are baby steps toward something far greater— becoming a self-sacrificing warrior. By allowing men to serve you, a woman, you allow a man to be a man. By allowing a man to be heroic, you fan into flame the essence of what makes a man William Wallace–like. Leslie allows me to "rescue" her often—I squash bugs on her behalf, I warm up the car on a winter's day before she gets in it, I get her a glass of water when she lies snuggled into bed at night, I make the phone calls that she dreads, I even clean the toilets (does it sound like I'm bragging?). The reason I love to do all this is

that she makes me feel like I'm her hero when I do. Leslie is of no lesser value by allowing me to fight certain battles on her behalf. In fact, in my eyes, she's of even greater value!

4. *Be an encourager.* Guys live off encouragement like a puppy lives off Puppy Chow. And the words of women hold a special power in a man's life. You could almost say that a man's sense of masculinity is directly proportional to the encouraging, man-making words spoken to him by the women in his life. When a young man's simple acts of valor are noticed by the female eye, and when the female voice utters such words as "Wow!" and "That was incredible!"—it's then that young males become men of honor. The encouragement of a young woman has the power to raise a man from the valleys of Dudsville to the mountains of Studsville.

As guys, we haven't been trained to protect femininity, we've been trained only to conquer it. But a Christlike warrior doesn't selfishly seek to *overcome* obstacles (such as women with morals). Rather, he *becomes* an obstacle that stands in the way of all forms of impurity and injustice. A warrior doesn't complain about sacred boundary lines— he gives his life to protect them. Don't settle for anything less. Help shape the men in your life into true Christ-built warriors, and you will help redefine manhood as we know it.

PART IV

tender
reverence

the passion

of a set-apart

young woman

His whispers are sweetness itself,
wholly desirable.

SONG OF SONGS 5:16, NEB

10

Cultivating Intimacy

Going Deeper with Your Prince

You will ask me, are you satisfied? Have you got all you want?
God forbid. With the deepest feeling of my soul I can say that I am
satisfied with Jesus now; but there is also the consciousness of how
much fuller the revelation can be of the exceeding abundance of
His grace. Let us never hesitate to say, this is only the beginning.

ANDREW MURRAY

NOT LONG AGO I sat in on a conversation in which some older married women were giving marriage advice to a lovely young bride-to-be.

"When your husband asks you to trust his judgment," offered one lady, "just try not to roll your eyes at him!"

"Yes, that's good," agreed another. "First turn your back, and *then* roll your eyes at him!"

After the chuckling died down, a wife of thirty years had a tidbit to contribute. "I know that right now you think marriage is going to be absolutely wonderful," she said, looking gravely at the glowing bride, "but you need to have realistic expectations. Husbands usually start ignoring their wives right after the honeymoon. So forget about happily ever after—soon you are going to have to work really hard just to get him to even notice you!" A chorus of hearty agreements followed this remark.

"Remember that you are marrying a caveman," piped up another lady, who had just celebrated her twentieth anniversary. "All men really care about is food and sex!" There came yet another round of laughter and emphatic nodding.

Though this woman-to-woman banter seemed playful and harmless, I couldn't help but wonder how this portrayal of marriage affected the bride-to-be. She was a young woman who had chosen to set her life apart and wait faithfully for her future husband. She had carefully guarded the purity of her heart, mind, and body for this one man. Was this dismal picture of married life all she could hope to experience? Was she doomed to be stuck with a mediocre love story once the honeymoon was over, living with a caveman husband who barely acknowledged her existence except when he wanted food or sex? These women didn't seem bitter or resentful about the way their own marriages had turned out; they were merely resigned to the fact that this was all marriage could be. They thought they were doing the young bride a favor by warning her not to set herself up for disappointment, as they once had, by expecting a happily-ever-after ending.

Don't Settle for Less

Before Eric and I were married, we heard a lot of similar advice about marriage. People cautioned us to not get our hopes up too high, to have realistic expectations, to understand that after the honeymoon phase we were in for a lot of disillusionment. And yet we had seen how the Author of romance had beautifully scripted every detail of our love story thus far—and we had to ask ourselves if there was any reason He would suddenly stop creating an amazing romance for us the moment we said, "I do."

About six months before our wedding, a couple who had been married for twenty-five years confirmed what we were feeling. "You may have heard a lot of naysayers out there telling you that romance dies after the honeymoon," they said, "but we want you to know that it doesn't have to be that way." The couple looked at each other fondly, took each other's hands, and then continued, "On our wedding day we were so in love—but here we are twenty-five years later and we love each other *so much more* now than we did that day. Don't ever settle for less."

Eric and I have always remembered that couple's profound statement—*don't ever settle for less.* We made a decision before our wedding day that Jesus Christ would always be the center of our love story and that we would always pursue deeper love and romance throughout our life together. That attitude has been the key to our relationship, and it has caused our intimacy to grow more and more amazing every year. Yes, it's true that building a strong marriage takes a lot of time and hard work, but when Christ is at the center, and when we aren't willing to settle for less than His best, it only gets more and more beautiful with time. Every day I am incredibly thankful that Eric and I decided to take the "don't settle for less" attitude into our married life.

As today's generation of young women, we have not been given much hope for the future. When it comes to singleness, marriage, femininity, or even a deeper personal relationship with Jesus Christ, we are often told, "This is all you can expect, so get used to it." In addition to what we hear, we are also affected by what we see. Our parents' generation is riddled with divorce, depression, and intense family conflict. Our own generation is filled with anxiety, abuse, eating disorders, and young men who are defeated by addictions, anger, and violence. And the statistics—on issues from divorce to violence to depression to eating disorders—are usually no different in Christian circles than they are in the rest of the world. It is no wonder that the majority of us have quite a dismal outlook on both our present and future lives.

But we do not have to live according to the mediocre standards of the world around us. Singleness, marriage, and womanhood do not have to be a dull, depressing drudgery. Those areas can be a little taste of heaven on earth, if only we will pursue the very best God has for us and never settle for less. The same is true about intimacy with our Prince. An amazing romance with Him does not have limits. There is always more to learn about Him, always more to worship in Him, and always more to experience with Him. On a daily basis we can take His gentle, outstretched hand and follow Him further and further into the amazing, boundless depths of a never-ending, heavenly love story. When our Prince is the center of our existence, the possibilities are fathomless. Life becomes an exciting, endless adventure. *Don't ever settle for less.*

SO FAR IN THIS book, we have discussed the *preparation* of our inner sanctuary: removing the trash and other lovers cluttering up our hearts and allowing our Prince to shape us into His lily-white likeness. We have also discussed the *protection* of our inner sanctuary: actively guarding what is sacred in our lives, actions, thoughts, and attitudes. But preparing and protecting our inner sanctuary is only the beginning of the amazing romance we can experience with our true Prince. There is so much more to be discovered in the inner sanctuary of intimacy with Him. Cultivating deeper intimacy with our Prince on a daily basis is what gives true meaning and purpose to our inner sanctuary. To stop short of this goal is like building a house but never moving into it or planting an apple tree but never tasting its fruit.

Daily, passionate intimacy with our Prince does not just automatically happen; it must be nurtured in order to grow. It is a lot like nurturing intimacy in a marriage. Eric and I had a wonderful time of intimacy the first week we were married. We expressed how much we loved each other; we spent every waking moment together, asking each other questions, trying to understand each other more and more. But did we truly know each other completely after one week of intimacy? Was our closeness in that week enough to sustain the rest of our marriage? What if, from that point on, we never spent any meaningful time together, never asked each other any questions, and never shared any experiences together? Our intimacy would quickly die. Our understanding of each other would gradually dissolve. To truly know and trust each other, we must continually and actively *nurture* our intimacy.

The same is true of our relationship with our Prince. So often we spend a short period of time focused on getting to know Him in a deeper way, but then we get distracted and the intimacy dies. Time goes by, and soon our understanding of Him comes from what we hear from other people rather than what we have *experienced* personally.

Have you ever noticed how most worship services are filled with solemn-faced, distracted people, singing along mindlessly, more out of obligation than sincere adoration of their Prince? Even in more expressive churches, I have talked with many worshipers who admit that they close their eyes and raise their hands simply because that is what is expected of them. I believe the lack of sincere and heartfelt worship we often see today comes from the lack of Christians truly *knowing* their Lord. Worship leaders often try to make the experience more enjoyable by adding cool guitar solos or smoke and lights on the stage. But mere entertainment can never replace true, heartfelt worship.

There is something missing in most modern-day worship—something I call *tender reverence* for our Prince. We sing a lot of songs about our own failures or desires, we shout out a lot of personal requests to heaven, and we may even get an emotional worship high by dancing, jumping, or clapping along with the beat. There is a time and place for having fun, singing little mindless ditties about taking a bath, or scratching someone's back. But how often do we tune out the rest of the world and stand speechless in wonder and awe at the incredible majesty of our Prince? How often do we sing about His incredible love and sacrifice with tears of gratitude streaming unashamedly down our faces? How often do we fall on our faces in adoration, stunned by His awesome power and amazed by His infinite tenderness?

I never understood what true worship was until I experienced deep, daily intimacy with my Prince in my inner sanctuary. When I truly began to *know* Him, suddenly I couldn't help singing to Him of my adoration or falling on my knees in awe before Him. Sincere, tender reverence for my Prince became a natural outflow of my intimacy with Him, not only in worship services, but also as *a lifestyle of worship* every day. Nurturing ongoing intimacy with our Prince produces an effortless outpouring of adoration for Him.

COME CLOSER

> *The [one] who would know God*
> *must give time to Him.*
> A. W. TOZER

We typically believe that going to church and reading our Bibles a few times a week equals a personal relationship with Christ. Most of us don't realize that deeper intimacy with Him can even be nurtured in the first place, and we don't know how to begin finding it even if we believe it is possible. Most of us would rather spend our time and energy focused on more immediate issues in our life—guy problems, friendship challenges, or weighty decisions that need to be made about our futures. And yet, amazingly, the answer to *every single issue* we will ever face can be found through deep intimacy with our true Prince.

This was something I began to learn not long after creating my inner sanctuary for my Prince. I had made several difficult choices in order to build my life around Him. I was living a very abnormal existence for someone my age. I wasn't following the recommended formula for success in any area of my life. Hundreds of nagging questions began to haunt me. *Will I ever get married? If so, how and when will I meet my future husband? What should I do with my future? Should I go to college? Should I pursue a career or a ministry? Will I ever find any close friends? What if I end up living with my parents for the next twenty years?* When I took all these worries and wonderings to my Prince, His response was simple and calm.

"Come closer to Me," came His soft, beckoning voice. I had been hoping for answers. All He gave me was a vague invitation. But there was something in that quiet invitation that intrigued me. I had taken many steps to live a set-apart life; now He was asking me to come even closer and learn more about Him.

But I wasn't sure exactly *how* to begin cultivating deeper intimacy with Him. The Christian world had taught me a few rules for living out the Christian life, and every once in a while they had thrown in a message about the benefits of a relationship with Christ. And yet when it came to building intimacy with Him, they hadn't offered much. I had memorized various scriptures as a child attending Vacation Bible School (the more verses you could say, the more candy you were given!). I had sung many songs about Jesus Christ in worship services—songs that declared "You are my hiding place" or "You are my all in all." But I hadn't stopped to ponder whether those lyrics reflected the reality of my relationship with my Prince.

As I felt Him calling me to come closer to Him, I asked Him to show me how to begin. He didn't present me with a complicated formula. Instead, He tenderly began to guide me into His presence, step by step. And as I drew closer and closer to Him, all the cares and concerns that had been haunting my mind seemed to melt away. *He* was all that mattered.

PRACTICAL STEPS FOR CULTIVATING INTIMACY WITH OUR PRINCE

Become a Student of His Word. I had always thought that studying the Bible meant flopping open the Scriptures, picking a one-sentence verse, pondering it for about three to five minutes, then mumbling a short prayer to make the study session official. The more sophisticated Bible studies I had experienced in Sunday school or youth groups weren't much better. Usually the leader would read a cool-sounding verse like "I can do all things through Him who strengthens me" and then launch into a fifteen-minute pep talk about how this meant we should always be sure to pray before volleyball games and big tests.

When I began to pursue deeper intimacy with my Prince, I realized that one of the best ways to get to know Him better was to get to know His Word better. Instead of just picking out a few random scriptures here and there to study, I decided I needed a much better understanding of the *entire* Bible as a whole. At first this was an intimidating prospect. The Bible was a huge book, full of confusing language that I didn't know if I could understand. A good deal of it seemed incredibly dry and boring. But it occurred to me that since every word in the Bible was a word scripted by my Prince, then none of it was unimportant—every page expressed a significant aspect of His nature and character.

I began to pour myself into the study of His Word. I realized that I needed to set aside far more than five or ten minutes a day to truly study the Bible. Even though I had to get up extra early, I began to devote at least an hour or two each morning to reading, studying, and meditating on Scripture. I found it extremely helpful to set goals for myself, such as working through the four gospels or making my way through the first several books of the Old Testament. I began to use multiple translations of the Bible so that I could better grasp the full meaning of what I was reading. For instance, I would first read the chapter in the King James Version, then go back and read it in the New American Standard Bible, and then once more in the New English Bible. Quite often, something I had not caught in one translation would come alive to me when I read it again in a different version. I also found it beneficial to use an exhaustive concordance (a book that defines the original Greek or Hebrew meaning of every word in the Bible). I would underline significant-sounding words in the verses I read and then look up their full meanings in the concordance. I was amazed at how much richer the Scriptures became when I began to understand the complete meaning of the words I was reading. Every time I opened the Bible to read, my focus was to gain a deeper understanding of the nature and character of my Prince. I grew so much closer to Him, and came to know Him so much better, through filling my mind and heart with His eternal Word.

There are many more layers of depth at which we can become students of the Bible: studying the cultures and time periods during which the words were written, studying the actual languages in which the words were written, and learning more about the art of effective observation, interpretation, and application of the words of Scripture. When you are ready, I encourage you to explore each of these areas to their fullest; the Bible is an endless frontier of depth and knowledge of our Prince.

Develop the Art of Journaling. When I was seven, I made my own journal using construction paper, a hole punch, and some blue ribbon. I think it was a summer camp arts-and-crafts activity. I was excited about my new journal and couldn't wait to start writing in it. A few days later, with a red crayon, I scrawled my first eloquent, though spelling-challenged, entry: "Today I got to go to the zoo. We fed the jirafs and a cloun painted my fase. Then we came home and ate makirony and cheez. It was the best day of my lif." (I have since tried to re-create the "best day of my lif" with a trip to the zoo, face painting, and a box of good old mac 'n' cheese, but somehow it just isn't the same when you aren't seven anymore.) That journal had four more exciting accounts of my incredible life at age seven, which I will spare you. But other than that one short-lived childhood masterpiece, keeping a journal was a foreign concept to me.

As I sought to pursue deeper intimacy with my Prince, I realized that often, when I tried to pray to Him or even to ponder what I had been learning in His Word, my mind would wander. No sooner would I be on my knees, asking my Prince to make me more like Him, than I would suddenly drift away into la-la land. About five minutes later, I would usually become aware of the fact that I had been writing out a mental to-do list for work, planning out what I was going to wear to a get-together that night, or wondering about the fate of the characters in whatever novel I had been reading. My tendency toward distraction was becoming a huge source of frustration to me. Then I read a book that inspired me to begin *journaling* the prayers, thoughts, questions, and insights I had received from Scripture. So I bought a simple spiral notebook and decided to give it a shot.

Instead of just saying my prayers, I began writing them down, like personal letters to my Prince. Suddenly, I was forced to find words to express the feelings, desires, fears, and ponderings of my heart rather than just allowing them to remain as vague, undeveloped ideas in my mind. I also began to feel closer to my Prince. Writing my prayers directly to Him helped me remember that I had a personal relationship with Him rather than seeing Him as a faraway, distant Being in heaven. Journaling also helped me to hear His voice more clearly by capturing on paper His gentle nudges to my heart.

For me, keeping a journal is still a crucial part of nurturing intimacy with my Prince. Every day after spending time reading His Word, I spend a focused period of time writing (or typing) prayers to Him: questions I have, sins I am repenting of, insights I've discovered, and direction or guidance I feel He has given me. The combination of studying my Prince's Word and personal journaling deepens my intimacy with Him in a way nothing else can. An added benefit is being able to look back over so many years of journal entries and see how faithfully my Prince has answered my prayers, gently taught me unforgettable lessons, and tenderly shaped me more and more into His lily-white likeness.

Discover Christian Literature. If you walk into most modern-day Christian bookstores, you'll find a lot of Christian self-help books, Christian novels, and works on Christian theology. There are plenty of wonderful things captured in many of those books. But I find it sad that today's Christian culture has, for the most part, forgotten the incredible strength and encouragement that can be found in reading about the personal spiritual journey of a life completely abandoned to Jesus Christ. When I first began to nurture deeper intimacy with my Prince, the books that were the greatest help to me along the way were Christian biographies. Reading about the struggles and triumphs and laughter and tears and valleys and victories of the men and women who had gone before me in this journey was both comforting and inspiring.

A huge frustration for many of us is the lack of Christlike mentors to help guide us in our pursuit of set-apart lives. Julie, a young college graduate from Michigan, recently told me of her frustration over this issue. "If I ever actually find an older woman who I really look up to," she said, "she is usually too busy to spend any time with me." Mandy, a college freshman from Washington, gave me her perspective on the dilemma. "Most older Christians do not have the kind of spiritual life I want," she wrote. "I don't see anyone's footsteps I really want to follow in."

The lack of Christlike mentors is a deficiency that I have felt keenly in my own life as well. But here is the good news: an incredible team of Christlike mentors *is* available to every one of us in the pages of Christian biographies. When I began to discover these kinds of books, it was like having my own personal league of mentors whom I deeply respected and admired. Through each page I read, these amazing men and women cheered me on, encouraged me, and gave me profound insights about living a set-apart life for my Prince. Whenever I found myself wanting to slip back into the mediocre existence of the world around me, these men and women reminded me not to settle, not to pitch my tent, but to keep pressing forward into the endless frontier of knowing Him.

Often the best biographies are not new releases; they are from quite a few generations ago. Remember that set-apart living is rare; it cannot be found in just any Christian life. Sometimes the best examples of people who reflect the lily-white likeness of our Prince can only be found in remote corners of dusty bookshelves or buried away in an old attic, like a long-forgotten but extremely valuable treasure map. Many of the best biographies are out of print, and some are available only through organizations that aren't always in the mainstream. You may have to do some digging, and you may have to read each sentence a few times to understand its older style, but finding these precious Christlike mentors makes the extra effort more than worth it. (A list of the Christian literature that has deeply impacted my own life can be found in the "Recommended Reading" section at the end of this book.)

CHAPTER TEN IN A NUTSHELL

How often we sell knowing Christ short. There is an endless frontier of discovery and possibility with our Prince, yet we stop at the outskirts of an endless frontier and convince ourselves that we've arrived at our intended destination. In reality, we've only just begun in our exploration of our Prince's kingdom. A set-apart young woman learns to never stop in her pursuit of her Prince. To a Prince's girl, every morning is the beginning of a whole new adventure in the great and unending love story. Every challenge is an opportunity to grow closer to Him, every triumph is an opportunity to praise Him, and every moment is rich with the privilege of loving and worshiping our precious heavenly Lover. If gold lies just over yonder, then, as heavenly miners, yonder is where we must go.

11

Confident Sparkle

The Unwavering Strength of the Set-Apart Life

> *I ask that God, out of His infinite supply of spiritual riches,*
> *would mightily supply your inner life with His Spirit's enabling*
> *power, so that Christ, your heavenly Prince, might make your*
> *inner sanctuary His sacred residence as you lean more and more*
> *on Him. And I also desire that you would be able to comprehend,*
> *along with all God's set-apart children, the extraordinary and*
> *life-altering dimensions of Christ's love. But even more than*
> *comprehending this love in your mind, I want you to know it*
> *experientially, deep within your heart, so that you may have every*
> *ounce of God within you that is humanly possible to have.*
>
> EPHESIANS 3:16–19, PARAPHRASE[21]

I DON'T EVEN know her name. But I won't easily forget the night that I observed the young woman whom I affectionately now refer to as the Coffee Shop Girl. For weeks after my encounter with her, her face kept popping into my mind. I couldn't stop wondering exactly who she was and what had shaped her into such a rare, authentic beauty.

It was a Friday night in March. Eric and I were sitting in an artsy little coffee shop, a popular student hangout not far from a state university. The place was packed to capacity. A local musician was performing, and dozens of college students were crowded around the little tables, drinking cappuccino, playing cards, chatting, studying, or hooking up. I sipped my chai and gazed around at the scene. The room was full of attractive girls and good-looking guys who eyed each other from across the room and then ended up at the same table, engaged in lively, flirtatious conversation. The students were acting like every other college group I'd ever been around—until suddenly I noticed *her*.

She was sitting at a table near ours, a bright-eyed, sandy-haired young woman who looked about twenty-one. To her left was a girl in a wheelchair who was unable to lift her head, use her limbs, or even speak. The sandy-haired young woman was softly touching the disabled girl on the arm, smiling and talking casually to her about the local musician's amazing guitar talents. At first I thought she might be some kind of nurse or aid for the girl in the wheelchair, but soon I realized that she was simply another college student, out on a Friday night with one of her good friends.

For the next hour, I stole glances at their table, intrigued by how they communicated back and forth, and especially by how sensitive and caring the sandy-haired young woman was toward her friend. She seemed to glow with an inward sparkle that exuded total peace and confidence. She was completely delighted to be spending the evening with the girl in the wheelchair, even though they made an unusual pair among the rest of the students. She appeared fully content to help her friend with her drink and chat with her about the music, oblivious to the flirting and hooking up going on all around her.

I found out later from Eric—who had chatted with her while he stood in line for a refill—that the two girls were roommates and that the girl in the wheelchair had been severely disabled since birth. The sandy-haired young woman spent much of her spare time helping her roommate with her day-to-day challenges, and the two had become close friends. Eric noticed that the sandy-haired young woman didn't seem to want to talk about herself, but she glowed as she went on and on about her roommate's amazing qualities—things that people often didn't notice because of the disability. Her sincere and sacrificial love for her friend was obvious.

As the night went on, this young woman fascinated me. She seemed to radiate an unshakable confidence. She could have easily blended in with the dozens of other girls there, but instead, here she was, joyfully pouring herself out to serve her roommate. In fact, she seemed to be having more fun than any other girl in the whole place. As the musician wrapped up his final set, I glanced out the window and saw the sandy-haired young woman whizzing through the parking lot on the back of her friend's wheelchair, the two of them laughing with childlike delight as they raced past the rows of cars. From all appearances, the Coffee Shop Girl had just had the best night of her life.

Though I never officially met her, I would venture to guess that this Coffee Shop Girl knows her true Prince in an intimate way. Radiance, confidence, and true authentic beauty come only from knowing Him and being shaped into His lily-white likeness. In the sparkling eyes and loving touch of this sandy-haired young woman, I saw the reflection of my Prince. I may never know her name, but the Coffee Shop Girl's example will stay with me for a lifetime.

THE APPLAUSE OF HEAVEN

> *By realizing the reality of our Prince within us, we are*
> *never bothered again by the fact that we do not*
> *understand ourselves, or that other people do not*
> *understand us. The only One who truly understands me*
> *is the One who made me and who redeems me.... It is*
> *a tremendous freedom to get rid of every kind of self-*
> *consideration and learn to care about only one thing—*
> *the relationship between our Prince and ourselves.*
>
> OSWALD CHAMBERS

It is all too easy to become consumed with trying to understand ourselves, with trying to figure out who we are and what our purpose in life is meant to be. And it is all too tempting to become obsessed with wanting the world to understand us and validate our existence. In this day and age of self-consideration, our society exhorts us to have plenty of self-esteem with inspiring statements such as "believe in yourself" or "be true to yourself." And yet the same society that encourages us to believe in ourselves also holds up unattainable standards of physical perfection in the form of flawless models and actresses who grace the covers of magazines or the screens of movie theaters. Our culture breeds insecurity while heroically parading a message of self-esteem. And whether we listen to the one voice and constantly compare ourselves against unreachable standards, or give in to the other voice and spend our energy trying to feel better about who we are, both scenarios cause us to focus on ourselves. Most young women fall into one of these two camps of self-consideration.

But in every generation there are a few who make other choices—like Amy Carmichael of Scotland, Esther Ahn Kim of Korea, or the Coffee Shop Girl of College Town, USA. What gives these young women their unshakable, confident sparkle? What makes them oblivious to the tyranny of social approval? What ignites them with courage to break out of the cultural norm and change the world by their example? The answer is simple: they have realized the incredible reality of their Prince. As Oswald Chambers would say, they have gotten rid of every kind of self-consideration and have built their lives around Him alone. *Their Prince is all that matters.*

When we are passionately in love with our Prince, we put Him above all else—not just in theory, but also practically, in every moment of our day-to-day lives. We do not live for the applause of the world but only for the applause of heaven. Our longings are not for people's approval but only for more and more of Him. We are marked by an effortless, unshakable strength that is found in the presence of our perfect Lover.

DELIGHTING IN HIM

Someone once told me that I could determine the primary focus of my life by where my thoughts went each night as I lay in bed, drifting off to sleep. I tried this little experiment when I was first trying to cultivate deeper intimacy with my Prince. I had created my inner sanctuary, I had built my life around my Prince, and I was spending focused time with Him each day. Surely, I reasoned, the primary focus of my life was my relationship with my Prince! But when I began to pay attention to what island of thought my mind drifted away to each night, I was startled to realize that very seldom did I dwell on my Prince. Usually, I started obsessing over relationships—thinking about different guys in my life, wondering if any of them could be "the one" for me, and trying to determine what they thought of me. Sometimes I thought about my future, worrying about where to go or what to do next with my life. Often I evaluated my appearance, personality, and social abilities, brainstorming ways I could change so that everyone would like me more. And other times I tossed and turned as I made mental checklists of all my undone tasks for work or school.

I realized that in spite of the fact that I had developed a daily relationship with my Prince, still it was *not* my Prince who consumed my heart and mind every moment of the day. If I had been in the place of the Coffee Shop Girl in a college hangout on a Friday night, I probably would not have been joyfully serving my physically challenged friend, unconcerned with what the world thought of me, and glowing with beautiful, unwavering confidence. Most likely, I would have been just like the majority of the other young women in that room—trying to fit in socially, attempting to make friends and be liked, and hoping to catch the eye of a cute Christian guy. It's not that these girls were doing anything necessarily wrong. Many were probably Christians, living upright lives of integrity. Some might even have focused, daily relationships with their Prince, as I did. But they, like me, were missing out on something so much more amazing, so much more beautiful, and so much more glorious—the art of rising above any form of self-consideration and attaining the unshakable radiance that comes from *delighting in our Prince* every moment of every day.

The entire reason for creating and protecting the sacred sanctuary within us is for the purpose of *enjoying* passionate, tender intimacy with our Prince each and every day of our lives. If a husband and wife created a beautiful haven of romance by cleaning and polishing their bedroom, setting the mood with flowers and candles, and jealously guarding their privacy, but they never actually entered the sanctuary to *enjoy intimacy* with each other, it would be a waste of time and effort. The same is true with our own inner sanctuary—it has been created so that we might truly delight in our Prince, experiencing unhindered, tender intimacy with Him.

When I began to pursue a lifestyle of delighting in my Prince, I wasn't entirely sure how to accomplish this in a practical way. It was so easy to delight in Him during my time of prayer, Bible study, and journaling, but throughout the rest of my day it was all too easy to become distracted and self-focused. I didn't see many examples of people who joyfully lived *each moment* for Him alone. It was around that time that I met Eric's sister, Krissy. She was unlike any young woman I had ever seen before. In her, I saw the same unwavering, radiant sparkle that I had read about in the lives of set-apart young women from the past. It didn't take me long to notice that her joyful glow and amazing servant's heart flowed directly from her intimate, passionate, moment-to-moment relationship with her Prince. When she sang during worship services, her eyes were closed and a huge, childlike smile of delight creased her entire face. She did not see the other worshipers, she did not notice the band, and she was unaware of her surroundings. She saw only her Prince. When she prayed, she poured out her heart to her Lord with trembling and tears and passion, totally unconscious of anyone else. When she spoke of her Prince, her eyes glowed with tender adoration and unashamed eagerness.

How does she do that? I wondered as I watched her. Her fervent joy seemed consistent every single hour of the day. After spending more time observing her, I began to notice that her communication with her Prince was not merely limited to her morning quiet times— she interacted with Him all day long, no matter what she was doing. Every day was an adventure with Him. Every day she expectantly watched and waited to see what He would do. She treated each person who came across her path as if He Himself had placed each one there. She kept her heart and mind open at all times, listening for His gentle, guiding whisper of direction. She could stop what she was doing at any given moment and instantly begin to pray or worship without a mental transition. She was overwhelmingly aware that her Prince was with her every second, walking beside her, whispering to her heart, and beautifully orchestrating the pieces of her daily life. She constantly acknowledged His presence. She never ceased to delight in Him.

Please show me how to have that too, I asked my Prince with a heart full of desire. Faithfully and gently, He began to show me how to walk through the day *with* Him rather than just walking through the day *representing* Him. I learned to inwardly talk to Him throughout the day—as I drove to work, as I interacted with the world around me, and as I drifted off to sleep at night. And I learned to inwardly listen to His soft voice, tuning my heart to hear Him throughout the day. From that point on, my daily adventure began. I was amazed at how exciting every day could be, even if I was simply going about a monotonous routine. When I learned how to continually communicate with my Prince, I truly learned how to live. I finally understood where true confidence flows from—the incredible delight of knowing that the most heroic, gallant, powerful Prince who ever existed walks lovingly beside me every moment of the day.

PRACTICAL STEPS FOR DELIGHTING IN OUR PRINCE

Here are some great questions to ask yourself: *Am I wholeheartedly aware, on a moment-by-moment basis, of the continual presence of my Prince? Am I able to speak to Him and listen to His voice no matter where I am or what I am doing?*

Getting to the place of delighting in our Prince throughout the day takes focused effort. We live in a culture that specializes in creating one distraction after another for our minds and hearts. There are a few significant decisions I personally made that helped me create a new approach to daily living *with* my Prince. I would like to share them with you now in the hopes that they will be a benefit to you as well:

Developing a Quiet Mind

When her ministry was at its peak, Amy Carmichael wrote about the importance of serving her Prince with a quiet mind:

> Having a quiet mind is not a question of choice—if we are to go on at all, we must have a quiet mind. All too many Christians break down, not because of their circumstances, but because of a weary, fretting spirit too rushed to dwell in peace.[22]

When I first read this statement, I found myself wondering how to maintain a quiet mind in today's world. From the time we are five years old watching *Sesame Street,* our society constantly throws nonstop action at us and trains our mind to never be still. From quick-paced television commercials to high-speed Internet access, our minds are used to moving at a breakneck tempo. The Christian world all too often follows suit. There are short books with one-paragraph devotionals and easy, one-minute Bible readings created especially for all the busy Christians on the go. When a group of Christians gathers, fifteen minutes is usually considered a long time to spend in prayer or worship, and frequently we fidget and restlessly check our watches the whole time.

I grew up allowing my mind to wander rapidly from one random thing to the next. My thoughts were easily distracted and hardly ever peacefully still, even during times of prayer, Bible study, or journaling. But when I began to pursue a daily lifestyle of continual communication with my Prince, I knew that something had to change. I needed to learn how to discipline my mind to focus on Him, no matter where I was or what I was doing. I needed to keep my thoughts still enough to hear His gentle voice. While drifting off to sleep at night, instead of just letting my thoughts wander aimlessly, I began to focus my mind on my Prince—either through meditating on a scripture I had memorized or just talking to Him about my day. After a couple of weeks of making a concerted effort to dwell on Him at night, I was surprised to notice that soon it started coming naturally. (An amazing bonus of this habit was that my sleeping became much more peaceful as a result of filling my mind with truth just before drifting off into dreamland.)

My next step was to discipline my thoughts in the mornings, just after I woke up. Instead of immediately making a mental checklist for the day or instantly turning on my CD player while I got dressed, I decided to try starting out my day by worshiping my Prince. This didn't mean a twenty-minute singing session—usually it just meant taking a few moments when I first awoke to kneel by my bed, focus on Him, and thank Him for His incredible love and faithfulness to me. When my Prince became the first thing my mind dwelled on in the morning and the last thing I thought about before falling asleep, it was far easier to continue to focus on Him and communicate with Him throughout my day. Eventually I was able to discipline my mind to dwell on Him on a more continuous basis—while driving in my car, interacting with people, or doing my work. Often, my conversations with Him were not elaborate prayers, just little statements of my love for Him or short prayers for His guidance in certain situations.

The more I learned to quiet my mind and focus my thoughts on my Prince, the more effectively I could deal with anything that was thrown at me throughout my day. As a result, I began to live a much more peaceful existence. When crisis or discouragement hit me, instead of being thrown completely off course with panicked thoughts racing through my mind, I became aware of my Prince's calm, steadying arms around me. When thoughts of my Prince were at the forefront of my mind, I was constantly reminded that He held the pen of my life, that He was scripting each chapter, and that He would never leave me. Eric has a saying that goes, "It is only when the waters are perfectly still that they can reflect the glories of the heavens." It is the same with us. Only when our minds and hearts are restfully focused on our Prince can we become reflections of His strong, steady, and unshakable peace.

Prayerfully consider some practical ways that you can train yourself to have a quiet mind on a continuous basis. Take notice of where your thoughts go when you are alone during the day or when you are lying in bed at night. These are excellent moments to begin developing different mental habits. Instead of letting your mind wander randomly, make a concerted effort to focus on your Prince during those times, whether it is by meditation on a scripture, singing a worship song, or just telling Him about what you are going through. As you face challenges throughout your day, remember to be aware of His presence at all times. Ask Him to assist you in conversations, guide you in decisions, and help you reflect His lily-white likeness no matter what you are doing. As you learn to speak with Him continually and open your heart to listen to His voice at all times, you will be amazed at how completely you will begin to delight in your Prince all day long. For "in [His] presence is the fullness of joy" (Psalm 16:11, NEB).

Cultivating a Heart of Worship

The more I began to cultivate intimacy with my Prince in my inner sanctuary, the more I realized that worship needed to be a central part of my daily life with Him. I found myself frequently wanting to fall to my knees and declare my gratitude, awe, and amazement for my heroic Prince. I had discovered a handful of worship songs that effectively expressed the adoration flowing out of my heart. They were songs that did not focus on my personal needs or desires. Rather, these were songs that focused only on my Prince—on His greatness, His holiness, His faithfulness, and His majesty.

Since worshiping privately was becoming a habitual practice, worshiping publicly came more naturally to me as well. I finally learned Krissy's secret of tuning out the rest of the world and simply adoring my Prince. I found that whenever I became upset, angry, or consumed with stress about something, the absolute best remedy for calming my inflamed emotions was to steal away to a private place for a time of worshiping my Prince. As my mind and heart were reminded of His splendor, His majesty, and His sacrificial love for me, my petty problems became insignificant in light of my heroic Lover. As I bowed in His presence, I was reminded that my life was resting securely in His capable hands, and I was filled with peace.

Think about your times of worship. Does your mind wander distractedly? Do you pay more attention to the catchy rhythms and cool melody lines than to the One you are singing to? Do you tend to gravitate toward songs that focus only on you—your needs, your struggles, and your desires? How often do you completely tune out the world and fall on your face in awe before your Prince's glory and majesty? How often do you unashamedly lift your voice to heaven and declare your adoration for your Lord? Do you have a true heart of worship for your Prince that lasts throughout the day?

It is a great idea to set aside a long period of time when you will not be disturbed and spend it in private, reverential worship of your Prince. Maybe you need to unplug your phone and turn off your computer. Maybe you need to dim the lights. Whatever it takes, it is important to remove any potential distractions. It's also important to choose songs that capture the beauty and wonder and majesty and glory of our Prince—songs that will help you truly worship *Him* rather than focus only on yourself. Another option is to read psalms or listen to a recording of psalms. As your mind and heart are filled with reminders of His splendor, holiness, faithfulness, and love, let the adoration in your heart flow out, unhindered, in your own unique expression to Him. Experiencing focused times of sincere worship helps us develop *lifestyles of worship* throughout our daily existence.

Learning the Art of Biblical Meditation

Earlier in this book I wrote about Scripture memorization as an incredible tool to combat the temptation to compromise the set-apart life. Scripture memorization fills our minds with truth. But it is crucial to take the truth that enters our minds and send it to our *hearts,* allowing it to shape our lives on a daily basis. That is where biblical meditation comes in. Before you start thinking yoga and incense candles, let me assure you that biblical meditation is nothing like the "become one with the universe" version of modern-day meditation that is frequently touted by yoga instructors, New Age guides, and leftover hippies. (Since I live near Boulder, Colorado, I have seen plenty of all three!) Biblical meditation involves actively pondering and processing truth until it becomes an integral part of who we are.

When I was seven, my Sunday-school teacher decided to award a special prize to the first person who could repeat John 3:16 word for word. She wrote the scripture on the chalkboard in huge letters and led us in a collective recitation of the verse, over and over. Dozens of little voices chorused these words: "John 3:16, For God so loved the world, that he gave his only begotten Son, that whosoever believeth in him should not perish, but have everlasting life, John 3:16" (KJV). I was the first one in my class to say the whole thing on my own without messing up, and by the time I left, I was the proud owner of a khaki-colored, miniature Pound Puppy, to the envy of all my friends.

I rushed home eagerly to inform my parents of my amazing talents, proudly demonstrating my unbelievable skill in Scripture memorization as I repeated the verse to them over lunch. Then came my mother's enthusiastic question, "And do you know what that verse means, Leslie?" I paused for a moment, thinking about the words I had just recited. *"God so loved the world"*—I pictured God looking down lovingly from heaven at the tiny blue globe of the world, like the one in the corner of my second-grade classroom. I guess I could understand His affection for His globe—I loved my Cabbage Patch doll the same way. *"That he gave his only begotten Son." Begotten* was a strange word. It sounded a little like *forgotten.* But how could God have a forgotten Son? God must not be a very good Father to forget that He had a Son! After evaluating the verse line by line, I finally came to the conclusion that it didn't make a whole lot of sense. But since I didn't want to appear ignorant, I answered my mom's question with a sure-fire winner I had learned in Sunday school—whenever you said it, you got the question right. Grinning confidently at my parents, I announced, "John 3:16 means that *Jesus saves!*" Based on their pleased expressions, I could tell I had gotten it right once more. But the reality was that though I could repeat the words verbatim, the meaning of John 3:16 was lost on me.

Most of us keep this same Sunday-school approach throughout our Christian lives; we may retain the words with our minds, but we never truly *own* the truth for ourselves. We know a lot *about* our Prince, but we don't truly *know* Him. When I began to create a lifestyle of delighting in my Prince, I found that biblical meditation was crucial to deepening my understanding of who He was and how He wanted me to live. Dwelling on the truth of my Prince until it became a central part of me created an ongoing attitude of adoration and worship toward Him.

The more I drew near to my Prince, the more I realized how infinitely deep, profound, and amazing His Word is. There is an endless supply of miraculous, powerful, world-altering truth in the pages of the Bible. It is like a map for buried treasure—to find the precious jewels takes focused time and energy. The Bible, though sacred and precious, is not the buried treasure we seek; it is just the map that leads us to the true reward, an eternity of intimacy with our Prince, Jesus Christ. The words of Scripture were not meant to just be quickly skimmed and easily digested—they were meant to change every aspect of our lives. To understand our Prince in His fullness, we must learn to *meditate* on His Word and make His truth an inseparable part of who we are as we study it, carefully examine it on multiple levels, mull it over in our minds and hearts, diligently pray about it, and apply it practically to our lives.

Developing a quiet mind, cultivating a heart of worship, and learning the art of biblical meditation are just a few practical ways that can help us develop attitudes of delighting in our Prince throughout the day. As we learn to walk through each day *with* Him, rather than just *representing* Him, we will become marked by an unshakable peace and unwavering strength—no matter what circumstances come our way.

A Picture of Set-Apartness

GERMANY, 1938

Betsy lay quietly on the hard wooden plank, covered with filthy, flea-infested straw, fighting back waves of nausea and claustrophobia. She lifted a weak hand to her feverish face. All around her, above her, and below her were hundreds of other female prisoners, crammed merci-lessly on thin plywood slats, piled so closely on top of each other that it was nearly impossible to breathe, let alone move. Images of her comfortable, inviting home back in Holland darted in and out of her consciousness like a vague, distant dream. How long had this nightmare been her reality? It seemed like years since she had slept in a real bed with clean sheets or taken a bite of warm, nourishing food. Her mind drifted back to the unforgettable day when she, along with her father and her sister, Corrie, had been arrested for hiding Jews from the Gestapo. Since then, she had been surrounded by inhuman torture, festering disease, and unspeakable pain and suffering.

After many long weeks in a dark and crowded prison cell in Holland, Betsy and Corrie had been packed into a dirty freight car along with eighty other sobbing, suffocating women and hauled to Ravensbrück, the dreaded concentration camp in the heart of Germany. For four days the women were crammed tightly against each other in the pitch-dark, sweltering car, without food or water, until at last the train halted and they were herded into the camp by screaming prison guards with submachine guns. Betsy and Corrie had been told that conditions at Ravensbrück were bad, but nothing had prepared them for this. Fourteen hundred women had been forced to sleep in a concrete room that was made to hold only four hundred. The bedding hay was soiled and rancid. Eight putrid, overflowing toilets served the entire room, and to reach them they had to crawl over rows of the overcrowded, sagging platforms that served as the makeshift beds. Shrieks and smothered cries could be heard throughout the room as several of the platforms came crashing down on the women below. The prisoners were exhausted and malnourished, and most did not share a common language. The sound of brawls, screams, slaps, and sobs echoed around the barracks.

Betsy felt a sharp pinch on her leg, and then another. The fleas were ruthlessly attacking. Beside her on the platform, Corrie suddenly bolted up, striking her head against the wood beam overhead.

"Betsy!" she hissed. "This place is swarming with fleas! How can we ever survive here?"

"Show us. Show us how," Betsy prayed aloud. Lately, the distinction between prayer and the rest of life had started to vanish. She was increasingly aware of the presence of her Prince, holding her hand, walking beside her each moment, and giving her the strength to persevere in the midst of such horrible circumstances. Even now, she felt a familiar, steadying peace creep slowly over her, like a cup of hot soup comforting a chilled body. Her Master was near. The sounds of agony and the smell of death all around her seemed to mysteriously fade. A soft, joyful smile crept over her face.

"Corrie!" Betsy exclaimed excitedly. "Our Lord has given us the answer! Find that verse in the Bible that we read this morning!"

Corrie glanced around quickly to make sure no guards were near. Then she fumbled through the pages of the tiny New Testament they had managed to sneak into the camp with them. In the dim light she squinted and whispered the words, "Rejoice always, pray constantly, give thanks in all circumstances" (1 Thessalonians 5:16–18, RSV).

Betsy's eyes shone. "That's His answer, Corrie! We can give thanks in *all* circumstances! We can start right now to thank Him for every single thing about this new barracks!"

Corrie just stared at Betsy incredulously, then looked slowly around the cramped, foul-aired room. "What can there possibly be to give thanks for in *this* place?" she asked skeptically.

Betsy paused, then smiled again. "Well, being put here together, for one thing." Corrie bit her lip and nodded in surprised agreement.

"And that there was no inspection when we entered—so we were able to keep our Bible," she continued excitedly. "And even for the crowded quarters, so that even more will hear when we are able to share the Scripture with them!" Corrie again nodded thoughtfully.

"Lord, we even thank you for the fleas," Betsy prayed serenely, but Corrie interrupted. "Betsy, there is no way that God can make me grateful for a flea!"

But Betsy was not to be deterred. She believed her Prince had put her in this place, fleas and all, and she was convinced that He had an amazing purpose for everything. As she drifted off into an uncomfortable sleep on the hard wooden plank, her heart was light. Her faithful Lord was at work in her life, and she would worship Him no matter what situation she found herself in.

Over the next few weeks, life formed into a grueling routine. Roll call came at 4:30 a.m. sharp, followed by an eleven-hour day of heavy labor as they listened to the bellows and screams of angry supervisors. But in every day there were a few moments of purest delight. At night, after a paltry meal of watery soup, Betsy and Corrie would make their way to the edge of the filthy room and gather around a dim light bulb for a time of worshiping their Savior. Soon a growing crowd of women began to gather for these reverential worship times. Life-giving truth was read from the New Testament, first in German, and then translated into French, Polish, Russian, Czech, and Dutch. Prayers were whispered. Hymns were softly sung. And gradually, life in the miserable barracks began to dramatically change. Before, there had been the continuous sound of brawling, sobbing, and cursing. Now the room buzzed with pleasant, considerate words and the sound of gentle singing. Betsy's reflection of her Prince had shone brightly and transformed the entire atmosphere of the dismal barracks.

No matter what happened to her over the next several months, Betsy kept worshiping her Lord with sincere adoration and a heart of serene peace. Though her body was chilled with fever, her chest heaved with racking coughs, and her limbs shook with weakness, she maintained a joyful, radiant spirit. One day a furious guard slashed her across the chest with a sharp leather belt for not working fast enough. When Corrie saw what had happened, she grabbed her shovel and rushed at the guard. But Betsy stepped in front of her before anyone saw the outraged action. "Corrie," she said quietly, "just keep working." Corrie stared in horror at Betsy's thin chest, now sticky with blood. "Don't look at it, Corrie," Betsy said softly, covering the wound with her frail hand. "Look at Jesus only."

"Look at Jesus only" seemed to be the theme of Betsy ten Boom's entire existence. Where others saw monstrous, animalistic prison guards, Betsy saw only lonely, wounded souls desperately in need of her Prince's love. Where others saw hellish, suffocating sleeping quarters, Betsy saw only the opportunity to reach more people with the truth of her Prince. Where others saw fleas, Betsy saw a gift from her Lord. Eventually, it was discovered that their nightly worship services would have been quickly thwarted were it not for the fact that the prison guards refused to enter their disgusting, flea-infested barracks for inspections. Even the fleas were a miracle from her faithful Prince.

Betsy ten Boom died in Ravensbrück. But during her life she impacted hundreds—both prisoners and guards—by her continuous adoration of her Lord, no matter what her surroundings. When her sister went to see her, just moments after she died, Betsy's eyes were peacefully closed, as if she were sleeping. Her face glowed with soft radiance. Her lips curved upward in a gentle smile. She had gone to meet her Prince. All her dreams had been realized.[23]

Today there are few examples of women who put their own trials and struggles aside to sincerely worship their Prince, no matter what their circumstances. It is all too easy to become consumed with our own pain, doubts, and fears and forget that our heroic Lord is standing beside us, holding our hands, faithfully weaving all things together for His amazing purpose (see Romans 8:28). Too often we forget to adore Him, to thank Him for His incredible love and faithfulness to us. But in every generation there are a few who make

another choice—a choice to shamelessly, tenderly, reverently adore
their Prince, no matter what they are going through. And they are
filled with a matchless radiance that is not of this world. Are you willing to be one of the few?

CHAPTER ELEVEN IN A NUTSHELL

It is fear that keeps us from changing the world. It is fear that keeps our mouths shut when we know we need to speak. It is fear that keeps us sitting when we know we need to stand. And it is fear that keeps us from giving everything when we wonder if we will ever get it back. We fear what might happen, we fear what might not happen, we fear what people think, and we even fear what *we* think. We are locked within a cage of trepidation, but our Prince provides us with the key that finally frees us from the tyranny of social approval, the despotism of evil foreboding, and the dictatorship of insecurity—He provides us with Himself.

A set-apart young woman is marked by the imprint of Christ. She possesses a placid calmness. Like an oak tree in the midst of a raging storm, she remains unruffled by life's cares. She possesses a confidence that is otherworldly. She smiles at trials, laughs at challenges, and is undaunted by the thought of dying. She cares not whether the world applauds her life; her ears are attuned heavenward as she listens for her Prince's cheers.

As set-apart ones, our sole passion in every moment of every day is delighting in our Prince. The moon could turn to blood and the mountains could crumble into the sea, but nothing can separate us from the One who loves us. The world may fear, but we always rest in the knowledge that even our death is a doorway into His presence.

12

Preparing for Intimacy

Future Husband Application

My beloved is mine and I am his.
Song of Songs 2:16, NEB

*M*ELISSA'S SOFT BROWN eyes glistened with silent turmoil. Her hands trembled as she took a deep, shaky breath and attempted an apologetic smile. "I'm sorry," she said quietly, "but this is the hardest thing I've ever been through." She went on to tell me the sad ending of her two-year relationship with her soul mate, Nate. Melissa and Nate had been best friends since high school. While attending the same college, they began to feel that God was leading them into a serious relationship. After spending several weeks praying about it, they officially became a couple.

They had made a conscious effort to keep God at the center of their relationship, always trying to honor Him when they were together. They were extremely careful about their physical relationship, wanting to keep themselves pure in every way. They encouraged each other in their spiritual lives and did Bible studies together frequently. Nate always made her laugh and seemed to know intrinsically what she was feeling and thinking. Melissa began to open her heart to him more and more. He seemed like everything she'd ever wanted in a future spouse. About a year into their relationship, Nate brought up the subject of marriage. Though they were not officially engaged, they began talking about their futures as one. Soon Melissa began silently planning their wedding and their life together as husband and wife. She waited eagerly for the day that Nate would finally propose.

And then, one day, the phone rang. She picked it up, smiling excitedly when she heard Nate's voice on the other end of the line. But then she noticed that something about his tone was strained and awkward. "I've been thinking," he began and then launched into a carefully planned speech outlining the reasons why he felt it was time to call it quits on their relationship. Melissa felt her heart pound with shock and disbelief as reality slowly registered in her numb mind. Nate was breaking up with her. Nate, who had said he would always love her. Nate, who had said she was everything he wanted in a life partner. Nate, her best friend, her soul mate, the love of her life. Nate, who just months before had sparked her deepest dreams by talking about their future together. And now, suddenly, without warning, it was over. Just like that.

For weeks, Melissa walked around in a daze, hardly able to believe how drastically her life had changed. At night, deep, heart-wrenching sobs racked her body, and her sleep was filled with restless nightmares. She awoke each morning to a dark cloud of depression. It took all her willpower just to force herself out of bed and into the shower. As she went about her days, going to classes and interacting with friends, she was haunted by insecurity and loneliness. A whirlwind of doubts began to plague her mind: *Maybe I am unattractive. Maybe I am unde-*

sirable. Maybe no one will ever want to be with me again. Maybe there is something wrong with me that I don't know about.

"People always told me that if I kept God at the center of a relationship and kept my purity, I wouldn't get hurt," Melissa told me, her eyes filled with pain and confusion. "But if this isn't a broken heart, I don't know what is!"

🦋 COURTNEY WAS a petite redhead with a story far different from Melissa's. And yet the cutting pain I saw on her delicate face told me it had ended with the very same heartbreaking devastation.

"I had always said that I would wait for my future husband," she told me miserably, "but last summer I met Jeremy. I gave him everything I had to give. I found out too late that he only wanted to use me." Since Jeremy had walked out of Courtney's life, she told herself that she was nothing more than damaged goods. All of her lifelong dreams of a beautiful love story had been shattered. She became desperate to prove to herself that she could still be found desirable by the opposite sex.

Wounded and vulnerable, she jumped at the next chance she had for another relationship. Brad seemed different from Jeremy. He was tender and sensitive, and he didn't pressure her physically like Jeremy had. But the longer the relationship continued, the more insecure Courtney began to feel. She convinced herself that Brad would never want to stay with her if he found out what she had done. She knew her tattered heart couldn't take any more rejection. She couldn't lose Brad. His devoted attention gave her the emotional security she desperately needed. So she decided to seduce him. She reasoned that if he compromised his own purity, he couldn't judge her for throwing hers away. After several weeks of subtle manipulation, Brad finally caved. Afterward, Brad was plagued with intense guilt. He began to withdraw from Courtney. In a panicked frenzy, Courtney clung all the more tightly to what was left of the relationship, pursuing Brad as aggressively as she possibly could. But it was no use. Brad wrote her a letter saying he could not be with her anymore. He knew what they had done was wrong, and every time he was with her, he was reminded of his mistake. When she saw Brad for the last time, he was a broken, depressed, bitter shell of the guy she had fallen in love with.

Courtney's jaw tightened in self-loathing as she told me her story. "Not only did I throw away everything I had," she said bitterly, "but I manipulated Brad into doing it as well. I am such a horrible person!"

AUTUMN'S SHOULDERS slumped in defeat as she told me the story of *her* heartbreak. It was far different from Melissa's or Courtney's experiences, yet the ending seemed strangely familiar.

Autumn had always been a fun-loving, outgoing person, but inwardly she was plagued with insecurity about her appearance. Guys had never shown much of a romantic interest in her, although she had always had lots of male friends. Often Autumn found herself wondering whether or not she would ever have the chance to find love. When Mike came into her life during her sophomore year of college, she began to feel hope for the first time. He treated her differently than any guy ever had before. Whenever she spoke, he was genuinely interested in what she had to say. When he listened, he looked deeply into her eyes, as if he cherished her every word. He always greeted her with an eager smile and said good-bye with an affectionate hug.

One night when Mike called unexpectedly and proposed a midnight chat at a nearby coffee shop, Autumn's heart began to race with new excitement. Could Mike possibly be attracted to her? They talked and laughed for hours that night, and Autumn walked home in a happy daze. For the next few months, late-night trips to Starbucks and long, philosophical phone or e-mail chats were ongoing occurrences between her and Mike. Though he never verbalized romantic feelings for her, he seemed to show her in a hundred little ways how much he cared about her and how much he valued their friendship. Mike was nothing short of a gift from heaven. Autumn was sure God had brought him into her life. He was everything she had ever dreamed about in a future husband. She frequently dreamed of the day when their relationship would finally grow into something more serious. She was beginning to feel sure it was only a matter of time. With Mike around, Autumn's confidence level soared, and she woke up each day feeling energized and happy.

And then one moment changed everything. Autumn's phone rang one evening, and she picked it up to hear Mike's enthusiastic voice. "Come over to my place," he said warmly, "there's someone I want you to meet." Autumn's heart raced with anticipation as she drove to Mike's apartment. As she rang the doorbell, she felt sure that he was about to introduce her to his parents or other family members—the perfect indication that something was about to happen between them.

But when Mike opened the door, there was an attractive brunette on his arm. "Hey, Autumn!" he exclaimed excitedly. "Thanks for coming! I want you to meet Bethany, my fiancée!" Autumn stood frozen in total bewilderment. His *fiancée*? Slowly the realization of Mike's words sunk in. She forced herself to shake hands with the pretty, dark-haired girl in front of her. Her mind began to race. How was this possible? How could he do this to her? with all the time they had spent together? with all the sweet and tender things he did for her so often? How could Mike be in love with someone else?

As Autumn cried herself to sleep that night, images of Mike's lovely wife-to-be filled her mind. The girl's perfect figure and flawless skin made Autumn painfully aware of her own long list of physical shortcomings. The devastating reality was finally sinking in—she was not good enough for Mike. He had never been interested in her romantically at all. Her face burned with humiliation. She felt utterly foolish. Why had she even dared to hope he would be attracted to someone like her?

THREE DIFFERENT GIRLS, three different stories, one devastating ending—heartbreak. When it comes to romantic relationships, heartbreak is the common ending for all too many young women today. For a huge percentage of us, the devastating heartache and pain we experience is caused by giving away our hearts, minds, and bodies prematurely, like Courtney. For many of us, an ocean of tears could have been avoided if we had only kept our physical and emotional purity carefully protected. And yet, we make mistakes. We give too much too soon. The sacred gift is trampled.

Others of us, like Melissa and Autumn, make focused efforts to protect our hearts, emotions, and purity. We desire to keep God at the center of our love lives. We make decisions after careful prayer and consideration. And yet, in spite of our caution, our hearts are carelessly handled, dropped, and broken, like a priceless crystal vase in the clumsy hands of a toddler. Sometimes this kind of pain is even more difficult to work through. We feel that we made healthy, Christ-centered choices and still got burned. There are no easy explanations for this kind of heartache. But whether a broken heart was caused by our own doing or not, there is still only one place to go to heal its shattered pieces: into the tender arms of our Prince.

Healing the damaging effects of heartbreak is crucial to preparing for true, unhindered intimacy with both our Prince and a future spouse. Ironically, after experiencing such deep, emotional turmoil, most of us are not even aware that healing is an option. We are trained by the example of the world around us to shove our pain beneath the surface, swallow our tears, and move on. And yet, after such a devastating experience, we are never quite the same. Life may continue as normal, but an invisible, jagged scar is left behind, making us vulnerable and insecure. We are left with a need to be assured that we are not intrinsically unattractive or undesirable. The comforting words of our friends and family are usually not enough. Self-help books and magazine advice columns can only do so much. Only the enveloping security that comes from being adored by a significant other seems to satisfy our craving for affirmation. And yet after we have a heartbreaking experience, we are susceptible to being blinded by our own insecurity, making bad relationship decisions, and ending up repeating the cycle all over again. The damaging effects of heartbreak cause a large majority of relationship mistakes in today's world. It is important to realize that the place to go for healing is not into another relationship. True restoration can be found only when we entrust our wounded, bleeding hearts to the gentle, revitalizing touch of our heroic Prince.

PRACTICAL STEPS FOR HEALING A BROKEN HEART

If you have ever had your heart broken, recently or in the past, it is crucial that you allow your Prince to fully heal the traumatic effects of that experience before you can be ready for true intimacy—both with Him and with your future spouse. It is not a quick or easy process. It is like an improperly set bone; though painful, the bone must be rebroken and then properly set so that it can truly heal. And yet, if you let Him, your Prince is able to fully restore you, to completely mend each fragment of your fractured heart. The insecurity and doubt you have learned to live with can be replaced with an unshakable confidence and beautiful radiance.

Following are some practical suggestions for beginning the healing process. This is in no way meant to be a step-by-step formula for healing. We are all different, with different levels of pain and different healing needs. These are just a few practical steps that might help get things going.

Soul Searching. A great starting place is to prayerfully think through each aspect of the painful experience. The other person may have been the one who broke your heart, but instead of only focusing on his part of it, take a moment to look at *your* part. Ask God to show you if there is anything on your part that needs to be made right. Here are some good soul-searching questions to prayerfully ask yourself:

- Did I ever cling too tightly to the relationship for security or affirmation?
- Did I ever put the relationship before Jesus Christ?
- Did I ever rush ahead of God in making relational decisions?
- Did I allow my emotions to lead the way rather than allowing the tender whisper of my heavenly Prince to guide me?
- Did I ever give myself physically, mentally, or emotionally to the relationship in a way that did not reflect the lily-white likeness of my Prince?
- Did I knowingly entice the other person to compromise?
- Did I lash out in retaliation, verbally or otherwise, when the other person caused me pain?
- Do I harbor bitterness or unforgiveness in my heart toward the other person?

As Christ's Spirit brings things to light, it is a great idea to write them down. (If you have not done so already, I would suggest working through the steps for repentance and forgiveness in the "Inner Sanctuary" material at www.authenticgirl.com.)

Getting the Prince's Perspective. It can be an amazing step toward healing to spend some time focused on gaining our Prince's perspective toward you rather than remaining blinded by your own emotionally clouded view. Find a secluded place where you will not be interrupted, and make sure you have plenty of time. Do whatever is needed to quiet your heart and focus your mind on our Prince—whether you play soft music, walk in the gentle breeze, or watch the sunset. When your mind quiets down, read the tender words the bridegroom speaks to his bride, found in the Song of Songs, allowing your Prince to speak directly to you, His cherished princess. Your Prince knows everything about you—all the intricate caverns of your heart and soul. He knows every line and freckle on your face. He knows the number of hairs on your head. He knows all your imperfections, all your weaknesses. And He loves you. He cherishes you. He treasures you. You are precious to Him. The words of the loving bridegroom to his bride in the Song of Solomon are your Prince's very words to you. Instead of allowing the careless actions or words of others to shape your perception of who you are, allow your self-image to be shaped only by the reality of your Prince's sacrificial, unconditional, timeless love for you.

Another wonderful place to turn is to Psalm 139:13–16. As you read the beautiful description of how lovingly and purposefully you were created, be reminded how much He treasures you as His princess. You need to be reminded that no matter what anyone on this earth says or does to you, the King of the universe, the Creator of all things, the Ruler of the heavens and earth has said that you are valuable. To Him, you are priceless. He loved you before you were even born. While you were still in your mother's womb, He had an incredible purpose for your life. And He still does.

After filling your mind with this truth, prayerfully ask God to give you *His* perspective on who you are. Then ask yourself these questions: *How does He see me? What is His perspective on what I have gone through?* It is a great idea to write down any thoughts that come into your mind as you pray, or write down key phrases that stand out to you in the scriptures you read. You might need to repeat this process often, until you are no longer plagued by insecurity or haunted by feelings of worthlessness. Allow your Prince's perspective to become yours as well.

Talking with a Teammate. Another wonderful healing tool in your hands is to ask God to show you someone in your life who can help you work through any lingering pain you are experiencing after a heartbreak. Ideally, your teammate should be someone who was not involved in the painful situation, but rather someone objective, with an outside perspective. Your teammate should be someone you trust and respect, someone who has built her life around Christ, and someone who can respect your privacy. Often the simple act of verbalizing the pain you are going through can go a long way in helping you heal. It is important to be honest about the struggles you are going through. Don't expect quick-fix advice or surefire solutions from your teammate. Sometimes you just need someone to listen to your story, to cry with you, and to diligently pray with you as you walk through this process. If the pain and confusion from the heartbreak you experienced is seriously affecting your life, you might need to consider meeting with your teammate on a regular basis until your raging emotions have calmed. Having a trusted friend to hold your hand, be a listening ear, and serve as a devoted prayer partner can make all the difference in a time of intense turmoil. Since not all of us have these kinds of trusted teammates in our lives, another way to find a Christlike teammate is to work with a professional biblical counselor. Teammates are an incredible gift from God to offer hope, encouragement, and a healthy dose of our Prince's perspective.

RELATIONAL INTIMACY

Ask modern-day young women to define *relational intimacy*, and you'll likely get a myriad of interesting responses. Erin, a bubbly college senior, recently gave me her angle on its meaning. "*Intimacy* means having really good sex with someone, right?" she said with a sly grin.

Caitlin, a twenty-five-year-old teacher, had another perspective. "*Intimacy* is when you really connect with someone—like you can talk to them for hours and hours."

Monica, a recent high-school graduate, had still a different view. "*Intimacy* is when you are in a relationship that lasts more than a month."

There is so much more to true intimacy than a physical, mental, or emotional connection. True intimacy is one of the most beautiful and precious gifts God has given us. But in a world riddled with casual sex, one-night stands, heartbreak, divorce, and abuse, it is no wonder our perceptions of true intimacy are so often skewed.

True intimacy is the most incredible aspect of my relationship with Eric. It is not merely physical oneness. It is not just connecting on an emotional level. True intimacy is built on a much stronger foundation—absolute trust and total vulnerability. True intimacy is sharing life with someone at the deepest level, knowing someone completely, and being known completely in return. It is what keeps my love story with Eric alive with tender romance. I know him so well—every talent, every flaw, every quirk, every hope, and every desire. Yet I constantly pursue knowing him even more. There is always something else to discover. Eric knows me better than any human on this planet. And still he is always seeking to learn more about me. I can share my deepest longings, my secret fears, and my hidden thoughts with Eric. I can make myself completely and utterly vulnerable to him. I can offer myself to him fully—heart and body—and he treasures me as a precious gift. I trust Eric with every fiber of my being. I do not worry that he will take what I have given him and trample it in the mud. I do not wonder if his love for me will fade. He is a part of me, and I am a part of him. At the end of the day, when we lie in bed just holding each other, I know without question that he understands me and that he cherishes me, even if no words are spoken.

Because the primary focus of my life is intimacy with my Prince in my inner sanctuary, I am able to experience true intimacy in my relationship with Eric as it was meant to be—a reflection of my love for my Prince. I do not look to Eric to fulfill my deepest needs. I do not cling desperately to my relationship with him for my confidence or security. I find my reason for living not in my marriage but in my relationship with Jesus Christ. And as a result, I do not put unhealthy pressure on Eric to fill a place in my life than can be filled only by my true Prince. Eric does the same—he finds his purpose, fulfillment, and security in his relationship with Jesus Christ alone. This creates the freedom for us to have unhindered intimacy in our marriage. We are not focused on selfishly meeting our own needs through our relationship. We are able to give to each other fully and freely, mentally, emotionally, and physically, without worrying what we will get back in return. The intimacy we experience in our marriage is an overflow of the intimacy we experience with our Prince.

I am able to trust my husband implicitly and make myself absolutely vulnerable to him without fear because of the kind of commitment our love is based on. Although we enjoy a beautiful emotional and physical connection, both of those areas can quickly fade based on external circumstances. When one of us is sick with the stomach flu, believe me, our physical relationship is the last thing on either of our minds! When one or both of us has been through an especially disheartening experience in life, when we are angry or depressed, it is impossible to be flooded with gushy, lovey-dovey emotional sentiments toward each other. And yet, no matter what difficulties we go through, our love flourishes, our commitment lasts, and our intimacy only grows stronger.

Similarly, our Prince does not approach us with a "temporary relationship" mentality. He does not flirt with us, spend a little time with us to see how compatible we are, try us out for a weekend, and then dump us on Monday morning. He does not stick with us for five or ten years, then decide the relationship has gotten stale and leave us for someone else. His love for us is unconditional. It is not based on our performance. It is not based on our perfection. It is not based on fleeting emotion or feeling. It is based on His choice, His decision to be completely faithful to us no matter what—even at the expense of His blood. True intimacy can only be discovered with this kind of commitment at the core.

THE BEAUTY OF SPIRITUAL ONENESS

When Eric first came into my life, our friendship developed in an unusual way. Since he was five years older than me, the thought of anything ever happening between us did not really enter my mind. And since I had made a commitment to give the pen of my love story to God and live in complete faithfulness to my future spouse, I was not even pursuing relationships. Eric had a spiritual fire and a hunger for God that greatly inspired me. As I wrote earlier, after spending time around Eric I would usually end up on my knees in heartfelt prayer or poring over the Scriptures, seeking an even deeper relationship with my Prince. Eric was an incredible motivator and encourager as I learned how to build and protect my inner sanctuary. I learned much about my Prince just by watching his life.

After about a year of friendship, we began to sense that God was leading us to a future together. (You'll have to read our love story for all the details of how *that* happened!)[24] But going from a platonic friendship to a romantic relationship in a way that was honoring to our Prince seemed tricky. We had never seen a relationship that wasn't based on emotional or physical affection. Once we came to the decision to build a future together, the general expectation was that we would now become "boyfriend and girlfriend," start holding hands and kissing all the time, spend every spare moment of our time together, passionately declare our love to each other, and become totally emotionally dependent upon the relationship. But we knew God wanted more for us than the typical way of doing things when it came to romance.

Some wisdom from my dad brought things into a clearer focus. "To experience intimacy in its fullness," he told us, "it should be built in three stages—spiritual oneness, emotional oneness, and then physical oneness in marriage. It is important not to rush to the next stage until the previous one has been thoroughly established."

I thought about my friendship with Eric up to that point. While we had been extremely careful to keep our interaction with each other as a totally pure, brother-sister relationship, a spiritual bond had grown between us. Our conversations were centered on Jesus Christ—what we were learning about Him or how He was at work in our individual lives. We had studied the Scriptures together many times. We had written worship songs together. We had gone on mission trips together and had ministered to and prayed for people as a team. It had been a friendship completely founded upon our relationships with Jesus Christ.

As Eric and I discussed where to take our relationship from there, we both agreed that we didn't want to lose the amazing spiritual oneness that had already started to develop between us. We wanted our spiritual bond to grow only stronger and become the foundation for our entire love story. Sitting on a grassy hill one fall afternoon, we said a prayer for our blossoming romance.

"Lord, guard our emotions. May we not be led by our feelings, but by You alone," Eric prayed. "Please strengthen our spiritual intimacy during this first season of our relationship."

For the next year or so, we made it our focus to solidify our spiritual oneness before allowing other forms of intimacy into our relationship. It may sound unromantic, but it was actually one of the most incredible, exciting times in our love story. When we were together, instead of dwelling on emotional passion or physical desire for the other person, we spent our time discussing new truths we were learning in our spiritual lives. We read inspiring Christian biographies together and talked about how they impacted us. We read Scripture together and spent hours praying and thinking about how that truth should affect our daily lives. We dreamed about ministering together and talked about ways that God might use our lives in the future. We worshiped our Prince together around the piano. As a team, we developed the same spiritual convictions about how to live and act and think. As time went by, though we each continued to have a strong individual relationship with our Prince, we also began to have a mutual relationship with Him as a couple. Jesus Christ remained at the center of our love story.

Later, when we sensed it was the right time for our emotional oneness to begin to develop, we were aware of the solid foundation of spiritual unity at the core of our relationship. Even today in our marriage, emotional and physical oneness are simply an added bonus— they are not the basis of our love story. Though emotions can easily rush up and then come crashing down like a roller coaster, a relationship built on Jesus Christ remains steady, strong, and unshakable. Both emotional and physical oneness can be experienced in their most beautiful forms when spiritual oneness comes first.

PRACTICAL STEPS FOR SPIRITUAL ONENESS

Many of us begin relationships with the confident declaration: "We are building this relationship with Jesus Christ at the center!" But after a few weeks or months, we are often swimming in an unpredictable sea of raging emotions and physical temptation. Once a relationship is based on an emotional or physical core, it is very difficult (if not impossible) to go back and create a solid spiritual foundation. That is why the beginning stages of a relationship are crucial. Here are a few practical suggestions for building a relationship with Jesus Christ at the center.

Savor a Season of Friendship. Our culture has set a predictable pattern for beginning relationships. We are familiar with the routine: we see someone we are attracted to, our eyes meet, we conveniently end up in a conversation, we spend a couple of days or weeks flirting until one of us finally admits we'd like to go out, and we start an emotions-led dating relationship in which we always try to present our best side to the other person. Even Christian relationships tend to follow this pattern; the only difference is that we say Jesus Christ is at the center and attempt to prove that fact by praying together, attending church together, and putting a few boundaries around our physical interaction.

But when emotions are leading the way, spiritual oneness cannot be developed. When we are careening along on the unpredictable river of feelings, the current takes control and sweeps us in whatever direction it wants to. We are no longer able to allow our Prince to be in total control of the relationship. The other dangerous aspect to consider is that emotional oneness—at its peak—desires to be expressed through physical touch. When emotions are allowed to run rampant, physical temptation becomes all the more intense and harder to control.

The great thing about first having a season of Christ-centered friendship is that a spiritual foundation can begin to develop before those emotions ever get in the way. In a friendship, there is not as much temptation to present only our best side to the other person in hopes that the other person will like us. We are free to simply be ourselves. We are able to see the other person for who he really is—rather than a smoothed-over, third-date version of his real self. In a friendship, we can tell far more easily if we are on the same page with the other person spiritually by observing his life in an everyday environment, watching how he treats others, listening to the words he says, and noticing where he puts his time and energy. And if something more is going to happen in the relationship, we can allow our *spiritual* connection to draw us together, rather than mere physical or emotional attraction. Emotional and physical intimacy can be enjoyed at their fullest when spiritual intimacy comes first.

Keep an Open Hand. Emily, a college student from Maine, is struggling during her blossoming romance with Jonathon. "He is so perfect for me—exactly the kind of guy I've always wanted to marry, and I think he feels the same way about me," she told me. "But whenever a week goes by and he doesn't call, I can't stop obsessing over him, wondering if he fell in love with someone else. It's driving me crazy!"

As Emily told me about her raging emotions over her relationship with Jonathon, it reminded me of a similar experience in my own life. Not long after Eric and I officially began our relationship, he left for a missionary training school several states away. He did not have e-mail, a pager, or a cell phone while he was gone. The only way I could communicate with Eric for several months was through letters (which had to somehow be kept hidden from his overly curious roommates) and once-a-week phone calls via one of the few pay phones on his campus. Without the constant reassurance of his devotion to me, I began to worry that he was going to forget about me and find someone else. One Friday night I hung around the house, waiting expectantly for a call from him that never came. Even though there were plenty of reasons why he might have been unable to call me—from an unplanned team meeting to an extra-long line at the phone booth—I still found myself restless and unable to concentrate on anything else. My mind began to race: *What if he is losing interest in me? What if he met someone else? What if he changed his mind about our relationship?* I wandered miserably out to the backyard and sat on the porch swing. Silently, I began to pour out my anxieties to my Prince. In the middle of my internal ranting, I sensed a clear, calm voice speaking to my heart.

"Leslie, do you want My very best for this area of your life?"

My agitation quieted as I responded, *"Yes, Lord—I do want Your best. I want You to script my story."*

As gently as a spring breeze, my Prince replied, *"Can you trust me with Eric? Will you allow Me to do whatever I see fit in this relationship?"*

At that moment I realized how tightly I had started to cling to this newly discovered love story with Eric. Even though I believed that my Prince had initiated this romance, I had taken the pen back out of His hands. But now I was reminded of how incredibly faithful my Prince was. Why had I questioned Him? Why had I ceased to trust Him? He knew, far better than I, what was best for this relationship. If for some reason Eric was not the one He had for me, then I realized He had an even *better* plan for this area of my life, even though that was difficult to imagine with my limited mind. I closed my eyes and opened my hands.

Forgive me for taking the pen back into my own hands, I prayed. *I now offer it fully to You again. You may do with this relationship whatever You see fit. I will trust You with all my heart.* Peace washed over me as I spoke those words. My Prince was in control—not me. From that point on in my relationship with Eric, I focused on keeping an open hand instead of clinging to my own desires. My Prince knew best. And He was always perfectly faithful.

One of the best ways to keep Jesus Christ at the center of a relationship is to keep an open hand at all times. Whenever we start to cling too tightly to a friendship, a relationship, or even the desire for a relationship, we must take a step back, examine our hearts, and entrust the pen back to the Author of romance.

CHAPTER TWELVE IN A NUTSHELL

If we were offered an amazing love story with a gorgeous man that involved everything from tenderness to trust, most of us would jump at the chance. But if we were told in advance that it would eventually crumble in divorce, most of us would rather spend life all alone with our hearts intact rather than ride off into a sunset only to see our daydreams morph into something devastating. How can we guarantee that an earthly love story goes the distance?

As women, we were made for intimacy. We were shaped to love with abandon and fervor. We were designed to stand by our man until we breathe our last breath. We were created to deposit ourselves completely into One. As set-apart young women, we can both recognize and harness this reality. We happily anticipate earthly love, and we desire to be successful in this area of our lives. But as set-apart young women, we make our ambition not the winning of an earthly prince but the total deposit of ourselves completely into One—our heavenly Prince.

The magnificence of our design as women blossoms like a flower from a seed only when we touch the ruddy cheek of our heavenly Prince. The amazing glory of womanhood awakens within us when we allow our Lord to gently caress our hearts. When we discover this divine intimacy within the depths of our female souls, we are prepared as young women to be set apart for the exquisite delight of earthly romance. We were each carefully and lovingly created to be a one-man woman. Extraordinary success awaits us when we are willing to learn the secrets of earthly love from the greatest Lover of all.

The Making of Poets

by Eric Ludy

Let's take a peek into the life of a young man named Chuck. According to most definitions, Chuck is not just your average burpin'-and-scratchin' male with high testosterone levels—in fact, he is a modern-day deluxe version of manhood and a popular nominee for many a young girl's Most Eligible Bachelor list. Take a look at his résumé…

Chuck is a leader in a student outreach ministry at his college, and he's a "save sex 'til marriage" dude. He has a boyish smile that quickly charms all females within a ten-foot radius. "When he looks at me I just melt," a young woman from Chuck's Bible study was overheard saying just last Tuesday. For most girls today, that would be enough to sell them on Chuck as this generation's equivalent to William Wallace.

However, Chuck has a few problems that are important for us to discuss. Chuck, like other men his age, is a firm adherent to the one-thing-on-the-mind version of manhood and has practiced it with great dexterity for years. Pornography has been a vice of his for a decade now, and it has helped train him in the idea that the female body is for his personal pleasure. Chuck would probably be shocked to realize that he subconsciously thinks femininity is important only as far as it brings him enjoyment. But the fact that he would be shocked doesn't stop it from being true.

Chuck may be a step above the typical guy today, but he is a sad substitute for true manhood. His training in manhood has left him fully equipped to enjoy the opposite sex, but outrageously *ill* equipped to have the opposite sex enjoy him. His training in manhood has left him terrifically well groomed to observe the outer shell of the female body, but poorly groomed to understand and serve the inner needs of a woman.

What If Chuck Gets Married?

If you take our young man, Chuck, and train him to have one thing on his mind, train him to place the interests and needs of women beneath his own, and train him to be insensitive to, or even unaware of, the unique demands of femininity—then what exactly happens to Chuck after he utters the words "I do"? Does Chuck, our newly married man, rise to the challenge that marriage offers, change his ways, and learn to be a great man? Or does our pal, Chuck, entrench himself even deeper into his trained ways of manhood?

Unfortunately, we are not hearing many married men today stand up and say, "Wow! I just love marriage!" We seem to only hear complaints.

To give an example of what most Chucks become, listen to this example: one of the number-one complaints of married men today, and this includes Christian men, is that they are not fulfilled sexually. Simply put, the cry from men today is, "We want more!"

Ask a married man if he could choose between having either more relational intimacy with his wife or more sexual passion in the bedroom, what would he choose?

"What do you *think*?" was the chuckle-filled response from a twenty-seven-year-old groom of four years. As a guy, I instinctively knew what he meant by that answer. He was looking at me as a fellow member of the Boys Will Be Boys Brotherhood saying, "You know, Eric, that we men are only interested in one thing!"

A thirty-something groom whom I queried only laughed, as if to say, "Do you even need to ask that question?" Then there was the "what type of guy actually wants intimacy?" comment that seemed to be an underlying theme with nearly every guy I polled. I did have one witty groom who peppered my very unprofessional survey with a little diversity by answering, "Do you want the *right* answer or the *real* answer?"

I'm sure that if I asked every married man I came in contact with over this next month, I would find some surprising answers every now and again. But unfortunately for us modern-day guys, we are fairly predictable when it comes to certain things.

The tragic thing is that most guys are even proud to be so predictable. I'm sure that for you, as a young woman, pondering these things about modern-day manhood can be quite discouraging. But I want you to know that there is tremendous hope. First, there is a resurgence in Christlike manhood taking place throughout this emerging generation of young men. It will take time to develop, but a new fleet of Warrior Poets is being formed. Second, there is an inspiring resurgence of set-apart young womanhood awakening as well, in lives like yours, which provides hope that a radical reformation of manhood is on the horizon. Because as I've said, one of the dominant forces that determines the quality of masculinity in a culture is the quality of its femininity.

We, as guys, are in touch with our wants, but our wants are all wrong. We need young women to help us realize that if we altered our wants, retooled our approach to finding man-ness, and used a new map on our journey, we would end up with far more in our manhood than we ever imagined.

CHUCK REVISITED

Let's catch up again with Chuck, our young married man. Over the past five years of their young marriage, Candice, Chuck's patient and loving wife, has repeatedly pleaded with him. "Chuck, I just need more time with you, I need you to listen to me, I need for you to do sweet things for me." Chuck scoffs at such suggestions. According to his makeshift map, men don't do things like that. According to his map, his wife's body is for his enjoyment, and his wife should submit to his wants and his needs for sexual passion.

"Chuck!" I want to scream. "Scrap the map!" I want to grab Chuck, and the countless other Chucks out there, by the scruff of the neck and say, "Listen to the words of your wife! If you would simply listen, you would realize that she holds the secret key for you!"

A woman instinctively knows that relational intimacy needs to be the goal for a healthy marriage. When relational intimacy is found between a husband and a wife, it will naturally bear the fruit of increased sexual passion. Married boys are shaped into married men when they finally realize that the buried treasure isn't the act of sex. The buried treasure is knowing, loving, and sharing the most intimate aspects of life with that woman sleeping next to him every night.

Here is where it gets practical for you as a young woman. We modern-day Chucks are not just taking this cluelessness into marriage, we are also taking it into our relationship with Jesus Christ. Just as relational intimacy is what makes a marriage great, it's also what makes a Christ follower great. But Christian men are whining for the treasures of Christ's kingdom, wondering why God isn't entrusting us with more, and the whole time we aren't exploring the underground caves that would lead us to the buried treasure. We think the buried treasure is something that we receive from Christ, when in actuality, just like in marriage, the true treasure is knowing, loving, and sharing the most intimate aspects of life with the Lover of our souls. We don't understand intimacy with women, let alone the most important form of intimacy: intimacy with Christ. We need you as young women to help show us the underground caves that lead us to the greatest intimacy of all.

THE MAKING OF POETS

When you think of a poet, your mind may produce images of crackling fires, roseate sunsets, finely crafted phrases with rhyme and romance, rose petals strewn upon the floor, and a gentle, ardor-laden melody dancing in the air. While poetry is surely woven within the fabric of those images, a true poet is more than just a man who can write a poem with a pen. A true poet writes poetry with his very life. A true poet doesn't use poetic devices to con the heart of a woman but uses the beauty of all that is poetic to serve, cherish, and express love to the heart of a woman.

Just as a true warrior is not a conqueror of femininity but a protector of femininity, a true poet is not just a wooer of a woman's heart but one who knows how to nurture and plant love in a woman's heart. Simply put, a true poet is a man who knows how to be intimate with a lover—first and foremost with Christ.

The recipe for intimacy seems to be the opposite of what we as modern-day guys have been trained for as Love Chefs. Intimacy involves the blending of five very important ingredients: the ability to listen, the ability to be tender, the ability to enjoy the journey (move at Christ's pace), the ability to be thoughtful, and the ability to cultivate stillness. It's these five trained-behavior abilities that young men must begin to learn. Not just so that we are great with our future wives, but also so that we are great in our love relationship with Jesus Christ.

The process of becoming a great man is lifelong, but it is always constant when the Spirit of God is at the helm of a man's life. The important thing for you as a young woman is to catch a vision of *something better*. The following sections will help you understand how you can help us as men begin to move toward the Christlike poets that God designed us to be.

THE ART OF GUY-NUDGING

For a woman to train a guy to be a poet, she must learn the art of guy-nudging. Guy-nudging is very different from pressuring and nagging; it's understanding how a man works and blending that knowledge with patience, gentleness, and some serious creativity. Oh, and a dash of sweetness also goes a long, long way.

Leslie is a world-class guy-nudger. Very subtly she helps me gain ground in certain areas of my life, and the whole time I may never even notice that she is nudging. Guy-nudging, at its best, is undetectable.

For example, Leslie has known from long before we were married that I have an inexplicable phobia of water. I like looking at water, I just don't like being in it. I'm a boat guy—not a scuba guy. Les and I, even before our marriage, had many discussions about what may have caused this water weirdness. She realized quickly that my problem wasn't one to take lightly. It was a deep thing within me that had wrapped itself around my mind like an angry weed.

In one of my weaker moments, when we were first married, I confided in Les that I didn't *like* the fact that I was afraid of the water. I told her I needed help. I wanted to overcome whatever it was that paralyzed me, but I couldn't do it alone. But I added one more thing: "Please don't try to help me the way everyone else in my life always has—*it doesn't work!*"

Well-meaning friends and family members up to that point had tried the "toss him in and he will learn to like it" method. And then there was the old line I got from guys growing up: "Come on, Ludy! What are you? Chicken?" Neither of these methods worked. I needed someone to help me figure out what would work. I needed some serious guy-nudging.

One of my favorite things about my wife is that she is a student of me as a man and therefore knows how to empower me to take steps forward in new directions. So Les tried a method that was perfectly suited for me.

"Okay, Eric," she said very sweetly, "there is no one around. There is no one who will care if you can't do it." With that she tenderly handed me the red and yellow striped boogie board. "If you're ready, just walk into the water. Don't worry about getting your whole body in, just go in up to your ankles if you want. Okay?"

Like a little kid learning to ride a bike without training wheels, I stuttered, "Okay." I then began my journey through the hot sand to the ocean's edge, Leslie holding my hand the whole time. With Leslie creating an atmosphere in which I felt comfortable taking steps forward in this new and fearful direction, I discovered freedom in the water for the first time in my life.

It started with a hesitant trip into the waves that got me wet up to my ankles. Leslie was careful not to push me. She allowed me to go at a pace at which I felt comfortable and unpressured. She, meanwhile, was boogie boarding like a pro, acting like she wasn't noticing my progress. As I waded into the water up to my waist, she didn't give me the ol' "told you so" glance, but acted as if I were any other guy wading out into the water up to my waist.

As a man, I needed her to help create the atmosphere in which I could grow. But I also needed her to patiently, and without a hint of pressure, wait for me to take the steps forward. *I* needed to be the one to take the steps forward. Each of the steps needed to be *my* decision.

It wasn't but fifteen minutes after my original journey to the ocean's edge that I first put the boogie board underneath me and started floating around. After another ten minutes, I was attempting to ride some of the smaller waves. Once I got the feel, I spent the next hour complaining about the small waves and looking for the monster ones. I was actually comfortable in the water! I was enjoying myself! Later that night I whispered in Leslie's ear, "We're going to do that boogie-board thing again tomorrow, aren't we?"

Guys are changed by women who understand them. Guys are never changed by pressure and nagging. The art of guy-nudging is knowing how to make a man feel understood and appreciated for who he is. And remember, guy-nudging must be done undercover. If a guy sniffs out that you are trying to change him, he can tend to get rather stubborn. So, while disguised as a wallflower, assist him in taking steps forward by creating an unpressured atmosphere in which he will feel comfortable taking those new and terrifying steps. If a man's dignity is protected and if he feels like the decision to take the step forward is *his* decision, then it is amazing how many a young man will dip his toe into new waters. A poet's qualities can't be forced upon a guy, but through the gentle nudges of a Christlike princess, he will be inspired toward new heights he never knew existed.

PUTTING IT INTO ACTION

There are four practical things you can do right now to help young men train to be true poets.

1. *Be tender.* A girl being tender to a guy is different from a guy being tender to a girl. Tenderness is giving to someone else what they need the most in the moment they most need it.

It's getting into the skin of someone else, looking at life through the other person's eyes, and therefore meeting those needs the way *that person* needs them met. And, as we all know, being in the skin of a guy is very different from being in the skin of a girl. Guys are motivated and encouraged by very different things than are girls.

Again, the safest and best way to practice tenderness is on your dad and brothers. The way to find out what motivates a guy—and therefore what he might most need—is to study him and determine the two or three things that he enjoys investing his time and energy into. It could be basketball, it could be computers, it could be airplanes, it could be a million other things, but every guy has an interest and a place in which he invests himself.

Then watch him at work. Guys, for some odd reason, love to be cheered on and observed at their craft. If you show excitement for a guy's area of interest, you will gain a unique avenue into his life. A woman who appreciates a man's hard-earned skill is a woman a man will listen to. And if you compliment a guy after you observe him excelling at his craft, your words will work to help shape him as a man. Remember, the words of a woman have the power to make a man either a poet or a peon. Please use that power the way God intended it to be used and help us become princes.

2. *Be a guy-nudger.* To nudge a young man toward becoming a poet, you have to be covertly creative. The secret is in cultivating an atmosphere in which he will feel unpressured and unnagged, yet challenged to grow. Practice thinking of creative atmospheres in which a young man could take steps forward in the direction of becoming a poet.

As I've mentioned previously, if you have a brother, this is a great place to start. I know it doesn't sound very romantic, but brothers are a great training ground and safe to practice on. For instance, invite your brother on a date. Take him to a nice restaurant and gently nudge him toward treating you like a lady. Stop in front of each door, and if he doesn't open it for you, say, in your most genteel voice, "Aren't you going to get the door for me?" When you sit down to eat, sweetly ask him to order for you and, if he's willing, do your best to be excited about his choice. Throughout the night, encourage him as a young man and inspire him as a Warrior Poet. Even allow him to pay for the meal if he is man enough to offer. A great line to throw in somewhere during the night, right after your brother has done something admirable, is, "You are going to make a great husband someday!" If you say it sincerely, he will *never* forget those words. Just remember, allow the guy to take the step forward. If he feels pushed forward, he probably won't budge.

If you don't have a brother, ask God to show you creative ways to nudge your guy friends toward greatness. You may not be able to practice the above suggestions on guy friends without giving them the wrong idea, but there are plenty of safe and healthy ways to nudge guys toward Warrior Poet manhood. If you see a friend demonstrating an attribute of Christ, take the time to point out that quality. If he does something gentlemanly, let him know you appreciate it. The more you appreciate his positive attributes, the more he will be inspired to grow in those areas of his life.

3. *Be willing to be unappreciated.* Plain and simple, when a young man finally takes a step forward in the Warrior Poet direction, never say, "I told you so!" You may have played a huge role in his growth, but if he senses an "I told you so" attitude from you, he will tend to either go backward or close you off from being a part of the process from then on. To protect a man's dignity, allow him to feel that the step was wholly his. If he desires to give you credit, that's great. In fact, that would show even further progress in his man-ness. But don't try to force him to give you the credit. Remember, you are supposed to be an undercover guy-nudger, not a front-and-center guy-shover.

4. *Be a defender of masculinity.* Just as you need young men to stand up and fight for authentic, God-designed femininity, guys need *you* to stand up and fight for authentic God-designed masculinity. In a sense, we need you to be female warriors defending the awesome potential of what manhood could and should be. Please don't punish manhood because of the idiocy of one or even a few. Manhood can be so much more than it is today, but we are spiritually weak and our true nobility has faded. One thing that will have tremendous influence on changing this is for young women to put on their armor like a Joan of Arc and come crashing into the battle to our defense. Great things are in store for our generation if you catch this vision. Manhood will once again rise from the ashes of compromise and will be something worthy of your highest affections—I believe that deep within my soul.

FINAL THOUGHTS

Warrior Poets, we would all admit, are rare these days. But the first step to their rediscovery is realizing that it is possible for Warrior Poets to reemerge. In these three studies on manhood, we have explored how you, as a young woman, can help that Warrior Poet formation become a reality in modern-day young men. We men are deluded into thinking that we are headed in the right direction. But burpin' and scratchin' within the city limits of Jerksville isn't what God had in mind. That is why we desperately need you to help us find something so much better.

It is my desire that you would catch the vision of world-altering womanhood, that you would be willing to sacrifice everything you hold dear in order to come away with your Prince. I hope you take the message of this book seriously and build your life around the creation of a sacred sanctuary for your heavenly Prince. There is nothing greater in all of life than to intimately share it with Jesus Christ—the ultimate Warrior Poet of all time!

Epilogue

In Every Generation

$\mathcal{I}$N EVERY GENERATION, a few young women discover passionate, daily, unhindered intimacy with their true Prince, Jesus Christ. Just like the princesses in our childhood fairy tales, once they meet this Prince and realize His incredible love for them, they *willingly give up everything else* to follow Him to the ends of the earth. They live lives with their Prince that are utterly different from the world around them. They are radiant. They are confident. They are fulfilled. They possess an authentic beauty that flows from within. They are world changers. They are set apart in complete and utter devotion to their Prince. And they stand out from among all other young women like lilies among thorns.

My challenge to you is to become one of those few in *this* generation: a set-apart young woman who allows the passionate intimacy she experiences with her Prince to completely transform every other area of her life. This kind of fairy-tale romance between a young woman and her true Prince does not come without sacrifice. It does not come without pain. But it is the most priceless gift we will ever be offered. And it is the most beautiful, fulfilling existence we could ever know or imagine.

As we seek to live the set-apart life, we will not likely be understood or appreciated by the world around us, often even the Christian world. But we are not on this journey alone. Our heroic Prince is with us. He is tenderly shaping us into His princesses—lilies among thorns in this generation. In His presence is the fullness of joy. Let's live for His applause alone.

"Trust Me, My child," He says. "Trust Me with a fuller abandon than you ever have before. Trust Me, as minute succeeds minute, every day of your life, for as long as you live. And if you become conscious of anything hindering our relationship, do not hurt Me by turning away from Me. Draw all the closer to Me, come, run to Me. Allow Me to hide you, to protect you, even from yourself. Tell Me your deepest cares, your every trouble. Trust Me to keep My hand upon you. I will never leave you. I will shape you, mold you, and perfect you. Do not fear, O child of My love, do not fear. I love you."

AMY CARMICHAEL[25]

Notes

1. Adapted from Charles Spurgeon, "A Bundle of Myrrh," www.spurgeongems.org, vol. 10–12, sermon number 558.
2. "Then Jesus said to His disciples, 'If anyone wishes to come after Me, he must deny himself, and take up his cross and follow me'" (Matthew 16:24).
3. "I have been crucified with Christ; and it is no longer I who live, but Christ lives in me; and the life which I now live in the flesh I live by faith in the Son of God, who loved me and gave Himself up for me" (Galatians 2:20).
4. "Or do you not know that your body is a temple of the Holy Spirit who is in you, whom you have from God, and that you are not your own?" (1 Corinthians 6:19).
5. "Now those who belong to Christ Jesus have crucified the flesh with its passions and desires" (Galatians 5:24).
6. "So then, none of you can be My disciple who does not give up all his own possessions" (Luke 14:33).
7. "More than that, I count all things to be loss in view of the surpassing value of knowing Christ Jesus my Lord, for whom I have suffered the loss of all things, and count them but rubbish so that I may gain Christ" (Philippians 3:8).
8. Eric Ludy and Leslie Ludy, *When God Writes Your Love Story* (Sisters, OR: Loyal Publishing, 1999); Eric Ludy and Leslie Ludy, *When Dreams Come True* (Sisters, OR: Loyal Publishing, 2004).

9. Paraphrased from Elisabeth Elliot, *A Chance to Die: The Life and Legacy of Amy Carmichael* (Grand Rapids, MI: Revell, 1987), 31.

10. Amy Carmichael, *Gold Cord* (London: Society for Promoting Christian Knowledge, 1947), 3.

11. Elliot, *A Chance to Die,* 31.

12. Elliot, *A Chance to Die,* 38.

13. Paraphrased from Carmichael, *Gold Cord,* 2–3.

14. *Braveheart,* directed by Mel Gibson (Hollywood, CA: 1995).

15. "The mystery which has been hidden from the past ages and generations, but has now been manifested to His saints, to whom God willed to make known what is the riches of the glory of this mystery among the Gentiles, which is Christ in you, the hope of glory" (Colossians 1:26–27).

16. Mrs. Howard Taylor, *John and Betty Stam: A Story of Triumph* (Chicago: Moody, 1935), 7.

17. Portia Nelson, *There's a Hole in My Sidewalk: The Romance of Self-Discovery* (Hillsboro, OR: Beyond Words Publishing, 1994), 1–3.

18. David Wilkerson, *The Cross and the Switchblade* (New York: Berkley, 1977).

19. Esther Ahn Kim, *If I Perish* (Chicago: Moody, 1979).

20. "The woman who is unmarried, and the virgin, is concerned about the things of the Lord, that she may be holy both in body and spirit" (1 Corinthians 7:34).

21. "That He would grant you, according to the riches of His glory, to be strengthened with power through His Spirit in the inner man, so that Christ may dwell in your hearts through faith; and that you, being rooted and grounded in love, may be able to comprehend with all the saints what is the breadth and length and height and depth, and to know the love of Christ which

surpasses knowledge, that you may be filled up to all the fullness of God" (Ephesians 3:16–19).

22. Carmichael, *Gold Cord*, 40.
23. Corrie ten Boom, *The Hiding Place* (Uhrichsville, OH: Barbour, 1971), 180–84.
24. Ludy, *When Dreams Come True*.
25. Paraphrased from Amy Carmichael, *If* (Fort Washington, PA: Christian Literature Crusade, 1938), 93.

Recommended Reading

Biographies and True Stories

Carmichael, Amy. *Mimosa, Who Was Charmed.* Fort Washington, PA: Christian Literature Crusade, 1982.

Deen, Edith. *Great Women of the Christian Faith.* Westwood, NJ: Barbour and Company, 1959.

Elliot, Elisabeth. *A Chance to Die: The Life and Legacy of Amy Carmichael.* Grand Rapids, MI: Revell, 1987.

———. *Shadow of the Almighty: The Life and Testament of Jim Elliot.* San Francisco: HarperSanFrancisco, 1989.

Foxe, John. *Foxe's Book of Martyrs.* Springdale, PA: Whitaker, 1985.

Green, Melody, and David Hazard. *No Compromise: The Life Story of Keith Green.* Eugene, OR: Harvest House, 2000.

Kim, Esther Ahn. *If I Perish.* Chicago: Moody Press, 1979.

McCasland, David. *Oswald Chambers: Abandoned to God.* Uhrichsville, OH: Barbour, 1999.

Richardson, Don. *Peace Child.* Ventura, CA: Regal, 1975.

Shetler, Joanne. *And the Word Came with Power: How God Met and Changed a People Forever.* Sisters, OR: Multnomah, 1992.

Taylor, Dr. and Mrs. Howard. *Hudson Taylor's Spiritual Secret.* Chicago: Moody Press, 1989.

Taylor, Mrs. Howard. *John and Betty Stam: A Story of Triumph.* Chicago: Moody Press, 1935.

ten Boom, Corrie. *The Hiding Place.* Uhrichsville, OH: Barbour, 1971.

Wilkerson, David. *The Cross and the Switchblade.* New York: Berkley, 1977.

Wurmbrand, Richard. *Tortured for Christ.* Bartlesville, OK: Living Sacrifice Books, 1998.

The Deeper Christian Life

Card, Michael. *The Parable of Joy: Reflections on the Wisdom of the Book of John.* Nashville: Thomas Nelson, 1995.

Carmichael, Amy. *Gold Cord.* London: Society for Promoting Christian Knowledge, 1947.

———. *If.* Fort Washington, PA: Christian Literature Crusade, 1999.

Chambers, Oswald. *The Complete Works of Oswald Chambers.* Compiled by Biddy Chambers. Grand Rapids, MI: Discovery House, 2000.

Cowman, L. B. *Streams in the Desert: 366 Daily Devotional Readings.* Grand Rapids, MI: Zondervan, 1999.

Edman, V. Raymond. *They Found the Secret: Twenty Transformed Lives That Reveal a Touch of Eternity.* Grand Rapids, MI: Zondervan, 1984.

Hurnard, Hannah. *Hinds' Feet on High Places.* Wheaton, IL: Tyndale, 1997.

Lewis, C. S. *Mere Christianity.* San Francisco: HarperSanFrancisco, 2001.

———. *The Screwtape Letters.* San Francisco: HarperSanFrancisco, 2001.

Tozer, A. W. *The Divine Conquest.* Wheaton, IL: Tyndale, 1995.

———. *The Pursuit of God: The Pursuit of Man.* Camp Hill, PA: Christian Publications, 1982.

Relationships and Womanhood

Elliot, Elisabeth. *Let Me Be a Woman: Notes on Womanhood for Valerie.* Wheaton, IL: Tyndale, 1999.

————. *Passion and Purity: Learning to Bring Your Love Life Under Christ's Control.* Grand Rapids, MI: Revell, 2002.

————. *Quest for Love: True Stories of Passion and Purity.* Grand Rapids, MI: Revell, 2002.

Shalit, Wendy. *A Return to Modesty: Discovering the Lost Virtue.* New York: Touchstone, 2000.

About the Author

LESLIE LUDY and her husband, Eric, are best-selling authors and speakers known for tackling some of the toughest relationship issues facing young people today. They have toured extensively, speaking to hundreds of thousands of teens, college students, parents, and leaders around the United States and abroad. Their passion is to motivate their generation to pursue a life completely transformed by Jesus Christ. Leslie and Eric have authored ten books including *When God Writes Your Love Story, When Dreams Come True, God's Gift to Women,* and *Teaching True Love to a Sex-at-13 Generation.* Leslie heads up Authentic Girl Ministries, a national fellowship for young women designed to encourage and equip set-apart femininity through conferences, discipleship groups, and resources. She and Eric live in Colorado with their toddler son, Hudson.

OTHER BOOKS
BY ERIC AND LESLIE LUDY

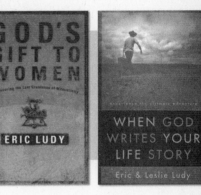

WHEN GOD WRITES YOUR LOVE STORY
Lay the foundation now—whether you've met your future spouse or not—for a lifelong romance that will stand the test of time. This book offers a whole new approach to building relationships...discover how beautiful your love story can be when the true Author of romance scripts every detail.

WHEN DREAMS COME TRUE
Be encouraged and inspired by Eric and Leslie's own love story—written in an engaging novel-style, about the decisions and mistakes they made in relationships before they met, how their friendship formed and grew, and the way God beautifully scripted the details of their romance. This story offers hope and vision for anyone in search of a love worth waiting for, and practical insight for those already in a relationship. It's a book you won't want to put down once you've started.

GOD'S GIFT TO WOMEN
- DISCOVERING THE LOST GREATNESS OF MASCULINITY
Wondering how to motivate the guys in your life toward Warrior Poet manhood? God's Gift to Women delivers an inspiring, candid, and practical message about the state of modern manhood and paints a powerful picture of what masculinity is meant to be. It's a must-read for today's guys and today's girls. It's a perfect gift for guy friends, boyfriends and brothers!

WHEN GOD WRITES YOUR LIFE STORY
Whether you're currently tackling major life decisions or simply longing to live a life that really counts, When God Writes Your Life Story will infuse you with vision and purpose. This book introduces the amazing journey that awaits us when we step into God's endless frontier. It showcases the heroic potential of the true Christian life. The God of the Universe wants to write your life story. And when He does, you mustn't expect a mediocre tale!